Dedication to the most important ladies in my life

The first lady, is my grandmother, Retha Taylor. She was a dedicated Seventh-day Adventist who loved her church as much as she loved the Lord. She was the one who taught me to iron and cook just so she could get me to sit long enough to plant the seed of faith within me. She would have the elders bring biblical movies to our home, which was the earliest form of Bible study.

The second lady, whom surely wore an invisible crown on her head, is my Sunday School Teacher Mrs. Evelyn Brewer. She broke off pieces of her life before us that we might examine the Christ that she knew. She remained our teacher for at least four levels through our adolescence classes.

The third lady, is my My Aunt Teeny. She was just a person that God had committed an assignment to periodically visit our troubled home. She sang as a tenor in our church choir, and she often sang lead to the song, "It is Well with My Soul." She was one of my mother's big sisters. As my favorite auntie, she would often bring me study Bibles and research materials (some of which I still have) long before my call to the ministry. She lived long enough to hear my first sermon as a Pastor, "Who Touched Me."

And finally, I give thanks for my wife Charlotte Brown-Parrott for her self-publishing knowledge and her commitment to the completion of the work.

Scripture quotations taken from the King James Version of the Bible.

Because of the dynamic nature of the Internet, any web addresses or links in this book may have changed since publication and may no longer be valid. Any people depicted in stock imagery provided by Getty Images or Adobe are models, and such images are being used for illustrative purposes only.

ISBN: 979-8-98801-86-05
Library of Congress Control Number: 2023912305
Cover Design by Charlotte Parrott
Editing by JLM Publishing

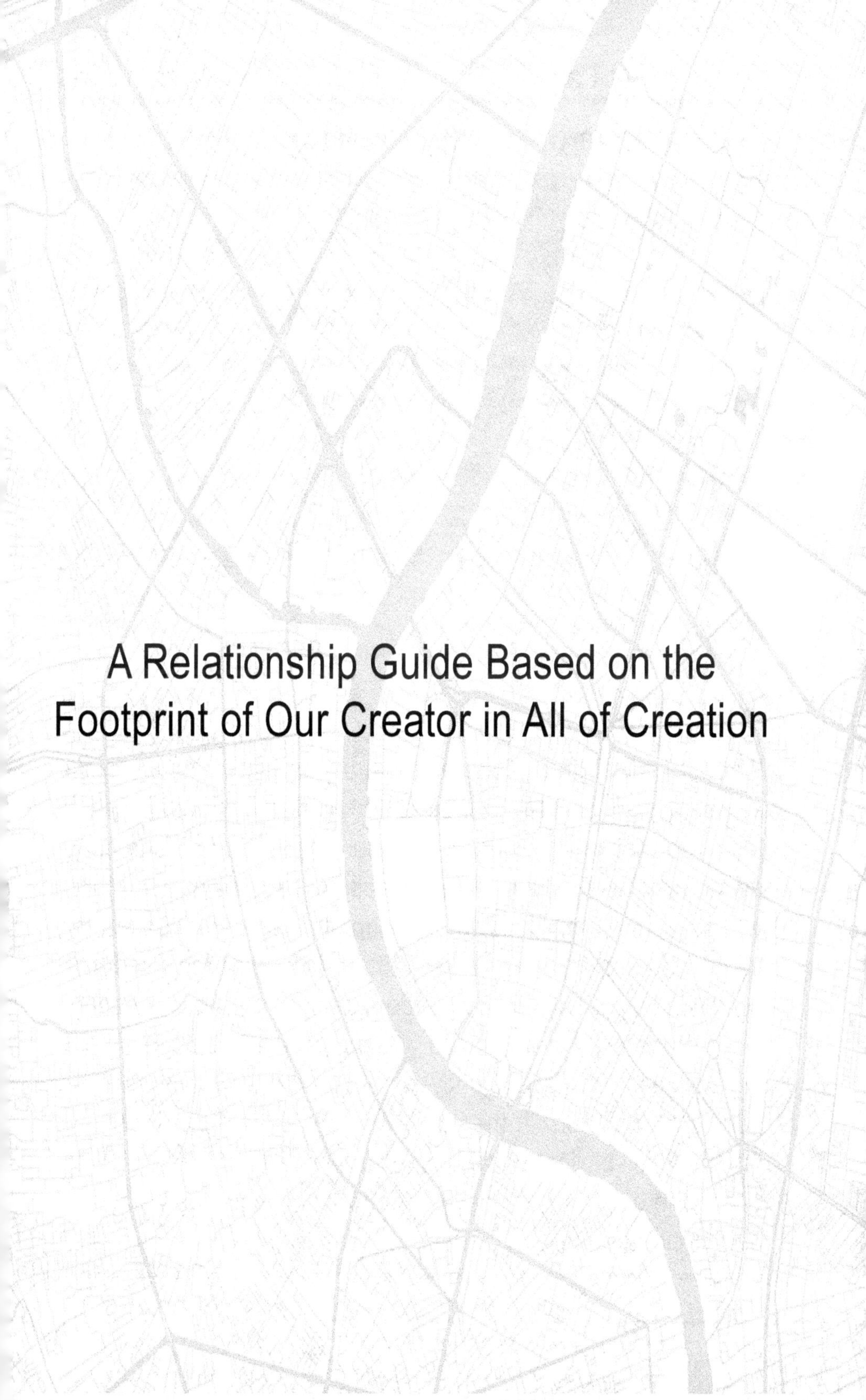

A Relationship Guide Based on the Footprint of Our Creator in All of Creation

The creative order and footprint of God

Introduction

Without biblical knowledge and instruction that comes with the awareness of pre-determined order and assignments, one is left to determine an order for themselves. In this free and equal society, that we as a people are rapidly becoming, each man, woman, boy, or girl does what is right in their own eyes leaving very little room for order or respect. In this so called, "liberated society," there is little or no considerations for lanes or boundaries wherein there are personal as well as societal restrictions. This mind of liberation (free agency) allows for the perpetuation of the spirit of, "whatever," in the minds and souls of each generation. This void of biblical knowledege and authority in our society, opens the doorways for each of us to be elevated to a status of person-hood-equality, wherein we trample over what had been established by man's Creator that we may exercise the assumed rights under no authority. It is this mindset that elevates each of us to our own authority, thus breeding chaos, disharmony, and heightened disrespect.

R. W. Parrott

The Biblical answers to the why and how questions that many are asking

- Whose assignment is it to be the head of the house with authority and headship (why)?
- What are the characteristics of divine leadership?
- Who is the spokesperson for the family?
- Does it matter who brings home the most money?
- What and why are there gender roles and not gender equality?
- Alternate life-styles and twenty-first-century concerns
- Sexual roles and attractions
- Personal responsibilities
- The importance of parenting

There is still an age-old question of the chicken and the egg; which came first? To those who believe the chicken came first, we must accept as fact that before the egg, there was a living form called a chicken. This chicken as the predecessor, and producer of the egg, was in fact the expected physical form of that which would eventually come out of the egg, "pre-defined." The chicken from which the egg comes, the hatched product, would have certain innate and physical characteristics. Like the chicken, the egg would become a feathered being with wings; that could not fly, having a beak and webbed feet, with reproducing capabilities (with both the egg and the seed), capable of reproducing rapidly in multiples, having an assigned purpose to supply a major source of food protein, known as poultry.

If we believe the egg came first, then we can reason that we too believe the egg was a kind of free agent; to produce "whatever." Creating the scenario that there was no pattern, no definition, nor expectation on the egg. A "whatever;" with no boundaries, limitations, or expectations until it hatched.

Each answer taken by itself, could be a topic of unresolved debates and endless discussions for centuries to come. Until, or unless, we introduce a variable, which is not a variable, but a constant. Either, when applied to the first question, how did the chicken get here, or how the egg got here; the corresponding answer suggests they both were created. If we follow the previously discussed train of thought, one expects or believes there is an "Intelligent being," a Creator, of which some know as God.

From the first chapter of the Bible, where God reveals Himself to us, we understand God created the chicken for His own plan and purpose. He created the chicken with the innate ability to reproduce itself in egg form. Thus, following the dictates of the Creator to reproduce after its kind.

AND GOD SAID, "LET THE EARTH BRING FORTH THE LIVING CREATURE AFTER HIS KIND, CATTLE, AND CREEPING THING, AND BEAST OF THE EARTH AFTER HIS KIND." AND IT WAS SO. (GENESIS 1:24)

Of course, this cannot complete the riddle until we understand both the chicken and the egg were not only created with innate restraints, disciplines, assignments, and expectations but also to answer a need, having purpose, definition, and boundaries. Therefore, that which hatched from the egg was expected to represent that which produced it.

What we sometimes fail to believe or understand is that all God's creation, especially mankind, bears the same creative footprint and signature as creation and the universe. All creation functions in a predetermined and pre-defined role: to fulfill its God-plan and purpose. There are certain requirements, boundaries, restrictions, and expectations on everything in God's created universe. Therefore, each of us has a God-plan, a predefined role in society that we refer to as "lanes." Lanes that in today's vernacular are referred to as our streets, roadways, or highways, which provide an avenue many travelers use to go in various directions while concluding different assignments, timetables and/or destinations.

In the same manner, there are assignments according to gender (male or female); their development in life (newborns or small children); their stages in life (teenager or young adults); and their positions in life or roles (mother, father, grandmother, or grandfather). Using this same thought process, we can deduce that there are assignments or lanes according to our gifts, passions, talents, and/or presumed chosen or assigned occupations.

Man: Husband, Father, Stabilizer, Teacher, Trainer, Provider, Leader, Head of the Home, Priest of the Family, Protector

Next-generation: their role is to learn and to acknowledge the wisdom of their parents and the elderly.

Relationships across generations wherein there is wisdom and instruction to nurture our teens and provide examples of overcoming some of life's trials with strength.

Woman: Wife, Mother, Caretaker, Homemaker, Comforter, Nurturer

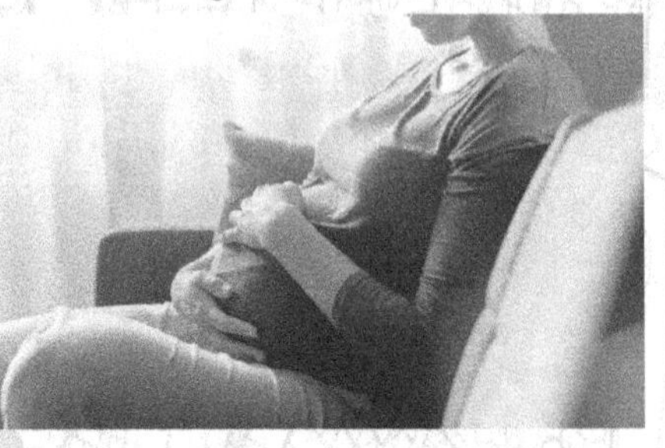

Protective roles: maintain society's peace, keep order, protect the weak, provide governmental stability

AS EVERY MAN HATH RECEIVED THE GIFT, EVEN SO MINISTER THE SAME ONE TO ANOTHER, AS GOOD STEWARDS OF THE MANIFOLD GRACE OF GOD. (1 PETER 4:10)

It is paramount that we understand we exist as more than merely travelers on this vast, wide-open, fast-paced, and multi-laned road called life. Each has an assigned lane in which we are born to grow, blossom, nourish, strengthen, complement, and/or complete our individual and collective preordained task or purpose. The most profound purpose for lanes is service. We are to impact, enrich, or enhance the lives of others as we serve in our preordained lanes. Each of us brings humanity a unique quality, flavor and/or disposition that meets and fulfills the needs of others, who, also having preordained assignments or lanes, are a predisposed way to impact our lives. We know this as societal elements, but the implications are much deeper and require a much closer look. Without the knowledge or recognition of our innately assigned and appointed lanes, as human beings, we become a bunch of, "whatever's," yielding only to our individual egos, ambitions, lust, fears, and/or pride; known for breaching, trampling, and/or violating the adjacent right-of-way of others.

As is evident in the disharmony, dishonor, distrust, and confusion in our relationship with each other.

Today, most live and function outside their divinely assigned lane. If we pause for a moment to explore the biblical record of creation, what came first is a no-brainer. Even before creation was created, there was a plan, and in every plan, there was a need or purpose, directives, and/or boundaries. From the beginning, "Then God said..." there was not only a plan, but also a sequential order to the things created. God left nothing to become a, "whatever." There is no place in God's order and creation for, "whatever's." God created based on a need to fulfill, bring about, or complete His ordained purpose.

Not only was creation made to fulfill a need, but because of the need, everything created has an identity with an assigned purpose and boundaries that, as intended, define its existence.

In the book of Genesis, we trace these principles and signatures.

The condition

AND THE EARTH WAS WITHOUT FORM, AND VOID; AND DARKNESS WAS UPON THE FACE OF THE WATERS. (GEN.1:2)

Creation based on God's plan and purpose

GOD CREATES LIGHT AND DIVIDES THE LIGHT FROM THE DARKNESS. (GEN.1:1-5)

Night and day, each having a distinctive lane, would define one complete day.

New Lane: Darkness would no longer have dominion in the universe.
Need: That darkness would no longer cover the face of the earth.
Definition: Night and daylight now define one day.
Boundaries: Day and night would interchange in a 24-hour period.

From the beginning, light is given dominion over darkness, clearly defining their individual and collective lanes.

Need: Light introduced and given an assignment.
Definition: Light, to illuminate the sky, to divide night from day.
Purpose: To define and appoint a giving day.
Boundaries: The sun to rule by day and darkness by night.

There was one universal element called water. And God divided the waters by bringing forth a firmament in the midst of the waters dividing the waters from the waters and he called the upper firmament heaven. (Gen. 1:6-8)

New Lane: To bring forth two separate waters from one.
Need: To establish a new domain within a new firmament.
Purpose: From the lower waters, dry land would appear.
Definition: Waters and dry land would occupy the earth below.
Boundaries: Waters and dry land would exist together.

God lays the foundation of His new order

It pleased God to divide the elements of the universe. One part above the throne of God, the other below the heavens. Lanes and boundaries were established in His great creation.

God restricts the boundaries of the universe surface water.

New Lane: The earth's waters made a place for the dry land.
Need: To restrict and appoint placements of great waters.
Definition: Great deep and powerful seas restricted to boundaries.
Boundaries: Waters to be gathered at appointed places on earth.

...And let the dry land appear. (Gen. 1:9)

New Lane: Waters made way for dry land, will hold their boundaries.
Need: That dry land be protected from the watery seas.
Purpose: That dry land would be prepared for the plan of God.
Definition: Called dry land, Earth.
Boundaries: To be above the seas and not overrun by the seas.

Lanes were defined, and setup to keep the waters from overflowing and vegetation appeared.

ON THE DRY LAND, GOD CALLED FOR GREEN GRASS AND VEGETATION TO COVER AND ADORN THE EARTH. (GEN. 1 :11)

New Lane: To bring forth food and vegetation from the ground
Need: To cover the earth, adorn, and beautify it.
Purpose: To provide food products for living creatures.
Definition: Vegetation, fruits, vegetables, herbs, nutrition
Boundaries: Plentifully, each after its own kind with the seeds

Here we can clearly distinguish the divine methodology, the "footprint of God." We can clearly witness the defined lanes and how each builds on the previous creation through our focus on the need, purpose, definition, boundaries, and structure as identified. Surely, a glorious plan is unfolding before our very eyes.

From these few verses in Gen. 1:1-11, we get our first glance showing what was to come was not an afterthought.

God's footprint further appeared...

And God said, Let there be lights in the firmament of the heaven to divide the day from the night; and let them be for signs, and seasons, and for days, and years: (Gen. 1:14)

And God made two great lights; the greater light to rule the day, and the lesser light to rule the night: (Gen 1:16)

New Lane: To provide a continuous source of light and energy.
Need: Harness the created light, nurture the earth, declare seasons.
Purpose: To illuminate the sky, both day and night.
Definitions: To mark signs of divisions: the days from nights.
Boundaries: Sun to rule by day, and the moon with stars by

night.

Lanes and boundaries of the sun and moon are clearly identified.

And God said, Let the waters bring forth abundantly the moving creatures that hath life, and fowl that may fly above the earth in the open firmament of heaven. (Gen.1: 20)

And God said, Let the earth bring forth the living creature, after his kind, cattle, and creeping thing, and beast of the earth after his kind: (Gen. 1:24)

...and God blessed them and said, "Be fruitful and multiply." (Gen. 1:22)

New Lane: The earth filled with creeping, flying living creatures.
Need: To multiply, bring forth life and fill the earth.
Purpose: There would be living creatures on all the earth.

Definition: Moving creatures, fowls of the air, creatures of the waters.

Boundaries: To populate the earth, seas, and the air. Each after its kind.

And God said, "Let us make man is our image, after our likeness: and let them have dominion over the fish of the sea, and over the fowl of the air, and over the cattle, and over all the earth, and over every creeping thing that creepeth upon the earth." (Gen. 1:26)

So God created man in His own image, in the image of God created he him; male and female created he them. (Gen. 1:27)

And God blessed them and said unto them, "Be fruitful, and multiply, and replenish the earth, and subdue it: and have dominion over the fish of the sea, and over the fowl of the air, and over every living thing that moveth upon the earth." (Gen. 1:28)

New Lane: Man created in the image of the Trinity.
Need: To be fruitful and multiply.
Purpose: To have dominion over everything upon the earth.
Definition: Male and female created he them.
Boundaries: Replenish the earth, and subdue it.

Each commissioned to multiply, reproduce and fill the earth, indicating how lanes are used to define species, territories, dominion, and the right to multiply. (Herein, is more information to determine which came first the chicken or the egg?)

As we explore the creation of the heavens and the earth, we find that a series of relationships have taken place. All of which were born out of either a causation of what was, a separation of what was, the change in what was, or the creation of what was not. Whether it was how, where, or why changes took place, at least two things have been constant: (1) a need for order and (2) a sense of harmony. With each change of creation, God set forth the path or boundaries in which each element was to operate and function in its sphere. The light overcame darkness and God confined darkness to a lane where it was no longer the dominant element, but now shares its previously dominated hemisphere with light. Light now shares dominion with darkness. However, light was granted the right of way in which darkness must yield. The waters were commanded to be separate, to make way for a firmament of which God created and calls heaven. These waters no longer have total occupancy, but have been called to be separate, one part above the earth and the other in a lane restricted with boundaries not to flow beyond its boundaries in the earth.

The water below, mostly, has been retained in deep and clearly carved oceans, rivers, lakes, and ponds, restricted to clearly marked lanes, and set boundaries where, in centuries, they have maintained their boundaries with land.

Vegetation was commissioned to cover the whole earth and given wide open lanes to adorn the earth with grass, herbs, plants, and trees with seeds after their kind.

And finally, birds, animals, and other creeping things were given unrestricted freedom; each to an innately defined lane to populate the earth and produce after its kind. God left none of these respective relationships to chance, and is the evidence that the vast and undefinable universe has order and harmony.

We know that creation has kept its commandments. Each element or component continues to operate in the defined and assigned lanes, just as God has spoken of their assignments. Otherwise, darkness would appear where there is to be light. The sun would have trampled over the moon, and the waters would have inundated the earth. Giving credence to the fact that each element obeys its God-ordained purpose, boundaries, and lane assignment, while recognizing the same as assigned to other aspects of creation. Without the recognition of each aspect of creation to their God-appointed lanes, the universe, as we know it, would have been in total chaos. As each element was established, multiple lanes were added regarding the outer edge of each entity's defined limits. Where one defined lane ended, a new clearly defined and marked boundary formed, creating the inter-connectivity necessary for new relationships to form between the previously created lane and the new one. Alleviating the need or opportunity for any of the elements to question: why am I here, for what purpose was I created, where do I belong as part of the creation story and in the total scheme of things?

The crowning work of all is God's creation of "Man." God formed man from His own image and likeness! A clay creature that would bear God's personal footprint and reflect His character.

As it relates to the way creation's record is revealed to us in the Bible, verse upon verse, each building upon the finished work of the other, we may have been led to believe that man was an afterthought of creation. Many believe God created the, "next thought," after recognizing each created entity was "good." However, the Bible reveals to us a God who plans the end from the beginning. God's finished work reveals the evidence of that which was divinely planned and ordained in His wisdom for His own good pleasure from the beginning, and supports the fact that God does nothing without a plan.

God told Abram that he was going to make a great nation from him; to accomplish this... the Hebrews were in Egypt for over 400 years under harsh taskmasters but left with over 1,000,000 people. (Gen.15:1-18)

In Genesis 37-42:9, Joseph's dream revealed that one day he would hold a prominent position, and his brothers would bow down to him. Out of fear or jealousy, Joseph's brothers sold him to a band of traveling merchants. Joseph lived an interesting life and even spent time in prison before the revelation came to fruition. Even in the lives of humanity, God has planned the plan, purposed the purpose, set the boundaries, and intentionally set their existence from the beginning. He worked out the plan according to His own good pleasure. As time is accomplished,

God brings about that which is already completed.

"The heavens declare the glory of God and the firmaments shows his handywork." (Psalms 19:1)

Nothing in nature was left to chance to become, "whatever." As He did with all creation, we find Biblical evidence of how God works out His perfect plan for humanity, giving them definition, purpose, and boundaries. Each creative step builds on, complements, and brings about a co-existence with all creation. It is through the same inter-connectivity that each created being was assigned a particular dimensional lane in which to operate, intending to impact the others of creation as it relates to the defined roles of their interconnected relationships.

"The Lord Almighty has sworn, surely as I have planned, so it will be. And as I have purposed, it will stand." (Isaiah 14:24)

If we pause and stand still long enough, we will see how each step is a sequential component of God's plan; to create an earth filled with wonder out of the darkness of chaos. A created place transformed from nothingness into a place where God would ultimately create a God-like being who would occupy, subdue, and have dominion over it. In all that our eyes can behold, and in all the mysteries that lay before us, we cannot help but marvel at the finished work of the creation which we have inherited as part of the promised birthright. Surely, the creation of man was not an afterthought, but the resounding purpose for each step in creation. When we consider the awesomeness of God, we too must say, as David did in the Psalms, "Who is man that God is so mindful of Him... that He rearranged the element of nature to prepare for him."

"That which may be known of God is manifested in us; For God has shown it unto us. For the invisible things of God from the creation of the world or clearly seen, being understood by the things that are made, even his eternal power and Godhead; so that we are without excuse." (Romans 1:19-20)

"When man considered the heavens, the works of thy fingers, the moon, and the stars, which thou hast ordained; What is man that thou art mindful of him? And the son of man that thou hast visited him, for thou hast made him a little lower than the angels, and hast crown him with glory and honor. Thy maddest him to have dominion over the works of thy hand, thou hast put all things under his feet." (Psalms 8:3-6)

AND GOD SAID, "LET US MAKE MAN IN OUR IMAGE AND AFTER OUR LIKENESS AND LET THEM (THE VISION OF MORE THAN ONE MAN) HAVE DOMINION OVER THE FISH OF THE SEA AND, THE FOWL OF THE AIR, OVER THE CATTLE AND OVER ALL THE EARTH AND EVERY CREEPING THING THAT CREEPS UPON THE EARTH." (GENESIS 1:26)

Man, the Image of God.

God's Image: Having the ability to create, design, engineer, give birth, procreate, orchestrate, give, and bring glory himself!
Man, the likeness of God.

God is man's maker and creator. All things proceed out of, from, and for Him. He is the supreme being of heaven and earth, and all authority rests within Him. In that authority and of His own good pleasure, God formed a lower being, and called it, "Man," who is fashioned as He pleased. God breathes His life force and power into man to animate him.

"...AND MAN BECAME A LIVING SOUL." (GENESIS 2:7)

We understand this was the breath of life, but it was much more than simply the breath of life. This in-breathing caused this clay being to come to life, to receive the, "Spirit of God," becoming a spirit being with a soul. This in-breathing was an essential ingredient for man to be made in the image of God. Man, therefore, was endowed with the attributes, nature, likeness, and the revelation of his creator, "God." This God-image, known before only to the Trinity and the heavenly host, is now revealed and exposed to man, from the breath He breathed into man's nostrils. With this in-breathing, God inwardly assigns, "pre-fitted," man to a, "lane," not previously given to any other existing, angelic and/or created being with the intent that man shall possess His image and be like Him (Genesis 1:27).

As we observe the image of God in creation, we must acclaim to God that He is the Supreme Creator. The One who can design, engineer, and/or give birth (to create) that which He purposes to be. The One who can procreate, orchestrate, govern, and rule over all that His word created and called into existence according to His good pleasure. God is sovereign over the heavenly host, and His dominion is without restraint or limit. There is great glory, honor, and praise that all creation should be attributing to Him.

Man, as the image of God, operates from God's perspective on the earth. He bears the heavenly image of God on earth. As God is in the universe and all things came forth out of Him, He justly and responsibly rules the heavens, and the earth, and all therein. God has given man, the male offspring of Adam, upon which the first commission and commandments were handed down, His mantle. This mantle passes from generation to generation with the responsibilities of manhood and the seed from within to procreate.

All things in the earthly kingdom will come under the precepts of the kingdom of God, as issued out of the governing dominion of man. The woman was taken from the body of man and formed in the image and likeness of man. As man was formed in the image and likeness of his creator, God, and answerable to God, so is the woman to man, as the woman came out of man. From the union of man and woman, Adam could procreate and bring forth sons and daughters to fill the earth.

As God is responsible for and governs over all that He has created, so is man's dominion on the earth. He is the overseer and watchman over all God has entrusted him with and to do. Through man, God desires to be known, clearly visible, and glorified on earth, as represented in Exodus 23:17.

"Three times in the year, all thy males shall appear before the Lord God." (Exodus 23:17)

As the condition of man grew worse and worse on the earth, God eventually took to Himself, and created in Abraham, a chosen people to exemplify and comply to His precept and concept that through Adam's lineage, He would reside with man. For this cause, God commands that three times a year, all the males of Israel, men, and boys, should separate themselves from all else and appear before Him.

Man's identity mirrors the likeness of God: his temperament, passions, ethics, moral code, resemblance in dominion, innate wisdom, and is only withheld from life eternal. As in the universe's creation, God identifies, gives purpose, and sets boundaries. As man is not a free moral agent, as humanity wants to be identified, he, man, is not left to do or become, "whatever," (what-so-ever he wishes). God has given him a definitive identity as the, "image of God," who is an earthly representative of the Godhead. As God is in the heavenly realm, so is man's responsibility on earth. In that, the image and directive of God gave man dominion; the likeness of God gives him purpose. In the same vein, the man after God's heart must possess the temperament of God and the passion of God for the things of God. As he bears the resemblance of God, he must also proffer the innate wisdom of God, and strict adherence to the ethics in judgment and the moral codes of God in justice.

Not only was man created to be a mirror to the Creator, but also the image of God in a three-dimensional body with a soul and spirit. His earthly responsibilities resemble that of God in all of creation that reflects the image of God the Father, God the Son, and God the Holy Spirit. Which speaks to man's three-dimensional relationship as a husband, father, and provider.

Man is to be in relationship with all creation, fashioned after his relationship with God, his Creator. Understanding his relationship with God far exceeds and precedes any other calling or responsibility. When we understand the relationship between God and man as it was before Adam fell, we clearly see there is no comparable relationship in all the universe, Heaven, or Earth. God, the Spirit Being, presents Himself as walking in the garden in the restful and peaceful time of the day, to spend quality time with Adam, the clay creature, as the omnipotent, omnipresent, all-wise, and all-knowing Jehovah. Representative of the one-on-one time between the Creator and the created that God still desires with His created today.

And they heard the voice of the Lord God walking in the garden in the cool of the day: (Genesis 3:8)

Man was created to be devoted to God, and committed to the things of God, while valuing their relationship above all others. Despite man's drifting and seeking his own sovereignty, God's calling, and connection beckons him back to an intimate time alone with Him. This connection will always represent the spiritual umbilical cord from the heart of man to the heart of

God. No matter how far away man ventures or fails in his first estate, the spirit of God cries out to man; "I am married unto you!" (Jeremiah 3:14) As it was after the fall, man needs to be reminded of the mantle he carries to occupy the lane in which God has prestigiously placed him.

"Return unto me and I will return unto you," is the story of Hosea and his wayward wife, Gomer. It represents the relationship between God and His chosen nation in Malachi 3:17. The satisfaction man seeks is only found in man's submission to God's will, plan, and purpose for him. Ironically, it is the God-image of sovereignty that man seeks to imitate as lesser gods in his fleshly pursuits that attracts him to the destructive forces of his adversary. The adversary, who he himself believed, could raise his horn above God and be equal to God.

Too many men have turned to their own ways, seeking to chart their own course apart from the ways of the Creator. This coupled with the lust of the flesh, and the lust of the eyes, and the pride of life, self-glory, (1 John 2:16), leads man to not honor nor operate within his God-ordained lane. The impatience and disobedience of man puts him outside the will of God, and man refuses to appear before God when he is beckoned to spend intimate time communicating with God. Man must "Humble [himself] ... therefore under the mighty hand of God, that He may exalt [him] ...in due time:" (1 Peter 5:6). Man's failure to understand the benefits available to him as the created of God, which affords him dominion over and access to everything God has created, which is already his for the asking; has resulted in his current state of disobedience.

CASTING YOUR CARES UPON HIM, FOR HE CARES FOR YOU. (1 PETER 5:7)

It is vital we understand the God-man connection and the fullness of what God has invested in His relationship with man. We cannot understand nor comprehend the fullness of the pattern for marriage, husband to wife, that God in his relationship with man has set before us. Man, as the head of all that God has entrusted to him, must emulate this relationship model in his earthly relationships: husband to wife, father to children, and provider for his family.

Husbands, love your wives, even as Christ also loved the church, and gave Himself for it. (Ephesians 5:25)

“For this cause shall a man leave his father and mother and shall be joined to his wife and they two shall be one flesh. Nevertheless, let every one of you in particular so love his wife even as He, Christ, has loved the Church. And the wife, see that she reveres her husband.”

The commandment of God to separate from all else and appear before Him was not solely for Israel, but for all men. It is imperative that men walk broad-shouldered under the mantle that mirrors the image and likeness of God. Man can only accomplish this by communing with God.

And hath made of one blood all nations of men for to dwell on all the face of the earth, and hath determined the times before appointed, and the bounds of their habitation; That they should seek the Lord, if haply they might feel after Him, and find Him, though He be not far from every one of us: For in Him we live, and move, and have our being; (Acts 17:26,27,28a)

Because that which may be known of God is manifest in them; for God hath showed it unto them. For the invisible things of Him from the creation of the world are clearly seen, being understood by the things that are made, even His eternal power and Godhead; so that they are without excuse. (Romans 1:19-20)

This assignment that all man has received from God is sure and non-retractable. All men will be held accountable for the charge and position he is born and ordained to walk in. When men forsake, desert and/or relinquish their, "assigned lane," as the keepers of the, "Godly order," in society, and the head of the family; ultimately, society as we know it is left without direction, stability, and/or the knowledge of order and purpose.

Further, as a husband, man causes others to produce. He watches over that which he has been charged with to promote and develop its strengths, and point out, direct and cultivate the areas of weakness, that all under his charge may thrive, grow, and be multiplied with the fruits of goodness.

I AM THE TRUE VINE, AND MY FATHER IS THE HUSBANDMAN. EVERY BRANCH IN ME THAT BEARETH NOT FRUIT HE TAKETH AWAY: AND EVERY BRANCH THAT BEARETH FRUIT, HE PURGETH IT, THAT IT MAY BRING FORTH MORE FRUIT. (JOHN 15:1-2)

As God toiled over His creation, man must toil over that which he has been charged with. These same godly attributes in man must be brought into his marriage, as husband to one woman, and father to his children. Man is jealous over all his possessions, as God is jealous over all that He has created.

FOR THOU SHALT WORSHIP NO OTHER GOD: FOR THE LORD, WHOSE NAME IS JEALOUS, IS A JEALOUS GOD. (EXODUS 34:14)

Be fruitful and multiply. His first assignment as a caregiver is to nurture, watch over, and cultivate all God has charged him with in the Garden.

As God Himself toiled over, formed, and placed His breath in man, He not only breathed into man a living spirit, but also His personality and power into man. God watches over man, and even in his rebellion, God embraces man, tutors, and directs his path with the storms of life, knowing His ultimate goal is to redeem man and all mankind back to Himself.

Who is he that condemneth? It is Christ that died, yea rather, that is risen again, who is even at the right hand of God, who also maketh intercession for us. (Romans 8:34)

As He disciplines us, His grace is sufficient to forgive us and restore us through His unmerited favor. Not even the angels in Heaven can claim the heart and passion of God as man can. Just as God has passed on to man His image and likeness, man is charged and positioned to pass on the gift of manhood and its benefits, responsibilities and roles to his sons, and the wisdom of God to his daughters.

Man is to be a confidence builder and a provider of strength and security for his offspring and for all humanity. As a father, man is the embodiment of a physical, spiritual, and physiological covering for those under his care. He is the stabilizer, fixer, and fastener of society, for which he must eventually give an account.

Before the creation of man, God toiled over His creation to create a suitable place for man to live and inhabit. He provided trees with fruit of every kind, vegetation, and herbs from the ground as a source of food and healing. Man, in his original state, toiled over nothing. His first assignment was to care for and appreciate all that God had created for him. The Bible describes it as a garden, but surely it was more than that! It was an incredibly special place, an intimate place where man could commune with his God and mature in his knowledge and confidence in the Creator as the Ultimate Provider. It was home, a place where trial, error, and mistakes would be expected, prepared for, and made. Of which, the consequences could be set aside in time, because God had already made provisions for man's needs and shortcomings. As God has provided for man, man must also provide for those under his charge.

Man must be a teacher and instructor in the ways of God. His most pressing desire should be that his family comes to the knowledge of their Creator, along with the need for intimate and prayerful communion with Him. Man must recognize his responsibility as the leader, peacemaker, and provider for his family, as well as his responsibility for the shaping of society. As he provides a home, he must create a space where love is felt and shared, and the commissary for his family's necessities. A place where his wife is nurtured, loved, accepted, and made to feel secure in her role. Together, they will be fruitful, and their offspring will grow in the nurture and admonition of God, confident that their needs will be met. The home is also to be a place of tender guidance and correction; discipline is to be provided in love, making room for growth and development, where mistakes are expected, prepared for, and made as they grow into adulthood.

Man's ability to dream dreams and see his dreams become his reality sets him apart from all creation. It is often the result of man's dreams that he provides for his family. As with God, a dream can originate with or without prolonged forethought. Like God, man can mentally design, engineer, fabricate, and/or produce the thing he has dreamed. In creation, we are told God toiled six days to prepare the universe for man; however, because 1,000 years are as one day with God, we cannot conceptualize how long God toiled in preparing the universe for man. But as it is with man, not only does he have the ability to dream and plan, but toil for years over a dream, refusing to rest until it is accomplished while not allowing his dreams to consume him.

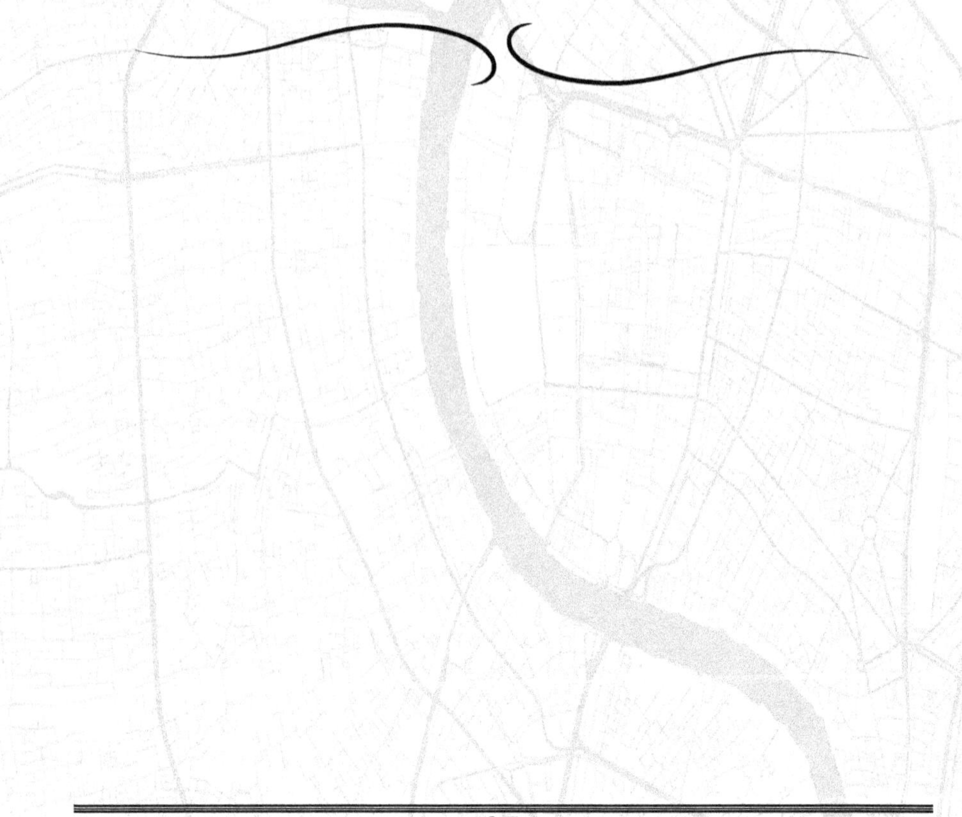

Man is a thinker and problem-solver who has wisdom for guidance. As demonstrated in the Garden of Eden, God brought all the earthly creatures, and Adam gave each of them names. God imparted to man the wisdom to know how to navigate, operate, research, explore, search out, separate, and calculate, often in a matter of seconds, what, when, and how necessary for him to do what must be done.

To fully understand man's dominion, we must operationally define dominion. Webster's Dictionary defines dominion as, "The transference of authority, as to lord over, the ability to subdue or bring into submission; to maintain order, discipline, and set boundaries." It is imperative that we understand that dominion was given exclusively to Adam, the first man, and, through him, transferable to all mankind. Adam, the forerunner, and the embodiment of God in man, who is formed from the dust or clay of the earth, is who God placed in the Garden alone, that he might till and dress it.

In Genesis 2:16-17, God gives Adam the commandment:

"...OF EVERY TREE OF THE GARDEN THOU MAYEST FREELY EAT: BUT OF THE TREE OF KNOWLEDGE OF GOOD AND EVIL THOU SHALT NOT EAT OF IT: FOR IN THE DAY THAT THOU EATEST THEREOF THOU SHALT SURELY DIE." (GENESIS 2:16-17)

It is the man, Adam, God visits in the coolness of the day as a part of the covenant relationship he and God shared. A covenant relationship that gives Adam dominion to be the keeper of the law and all that would eventually be charged to mankind. In Adam is the divine blueprint that is to be followed; but even more so, he is the first of the lineage of man who walks according to the order of this mantle God placed in Adam.

Just as there is an order to creation, there is an order to dominion and headship, which solidifies the principles that the formed cannot be greater than or equal to that which formed it. We can recognize this order of dominion and headship, first in God, then in creation, and Adam, out of Adam to woman, and then out of woman, and from the seed of Adam to mankind.

Unless we submit ourselves to the established order of creation and the created and return to a healthy respect or reverence of God, our society will continue to violate definitions and boundaries designed to give us clearly marked lanes of position, purpose, and order in our society. Lanes which identify every divinely set order of God's predestined plans and purposes, and who demand they be recognized, and respected. Godly defined order must be adhered to and carried out to achieve the full God-given agenda for life, the order of life, and eventual happiness.

As on our highways, bowling alleys and state roads, these societal lanes are the invisible markings of divine preordained assignments. It is here that we perceive the social right-of-way to lineage, the divine hierarchy of our social governments, subordinates, supporters, and how each of us as elements of our society must recognize the need for order, precepts, right-of-ways, boundaries and dimensions that will allow us to function individually and collectively as intended. Without lane recognition, every person is left to do whatever is right in their own eyes, basically to become a, "whatever," where each person, declaring personhood, will trample over what is esteemed by our Creator as just, due, and/or set boundaries and lanes appointed for others, violating God's ordained system of creative order.

As the sun, moon and stars are each element of the heavens, so are each of us as individual elements of mankind on earth. Each having earthly assignments according to the need, purpose, and boundaries/lanes, wherein we contribute to the welfare of society, fulfill purposes and our assignments, to meet the needs of our society as the established footprints left for us by our Creator. As God has left his creative footprints on the heavens with unquestionable order, He has performed the same on the earth and with mankind. His footprint brings to our relationships with one another, a sense of assignment and the value of our existence.

In the ultra-modern world in which we now live, and as we function under a politically-correct society, it has become offensive to declare one gender of mankind above the other. To fit this present-day mindset, we would prefer to read only the summary to (Genesis 1:27-28) instead of reading the scripture itself:

So, God created man in His own image, in the image of God created He him; male and female created He them. And God blessed them, and God said unto them, Be fruitful, and multiply, and replenish the earth, and subdue it: and have dominion over the fish of the sea, and over the fowl of the air, and over every living thing that moves upon the earth. (Genesis 1:27-28)

Many believe these verses refer to gender equality between male and female. However, gender equality is not consistent or in accordance with God's creative order, as discussed and verified in the sequential order or footprint of God, the Creator.

In keeping with the context of the biblical record, we find that only the animals, fowl of the air, and sea creatures are created male and female; simultaneously, given their identity, purpose, and boundaries as after their kind. This is still the case even within those species where the female is the hunter, and the male remains the dominant gender and leader.

And the Lord God formed man out of the dust of the ground, and breathed into his nostrils the breath of life; and man became a living soul. And the Lord God planted

a garden eastward of Eden, and there He put the man he had formed. (Genesis 2:7-8)

Mankind through Adam was given dominion over all the earth, superior to all the animals and creeping things on earth. The charge of a man with the responsibility to, "...be fruitful, and multiply, and replenish the earth, and subdue it: and have dominion..." is in keeping with the purpose for which Adam is created. However, man did not have the mate to complete this order until:

"...God caused a deep sleep to fall upon Adam, and he slept: and He took one of his ribs and closed up the flesh instead thereof; And the rib, which the Lord God had taken from man, made He a woman, and brought her unto the man. And Adam said, This is now bone of my bones, and flesh of my flesh: she shall be called Woman, because she was taken out of Man." (Genesis 2:21-23)

Mankind came from Adam through Eve, not only establishing a social hierarchy, but verifying the preeminence and authority of man. Reminding us, "...that which is made or formed cannot be greater than or equal to that from which it is formed."

Although (Genesis 1:27-28) supersedes the 2nd chapter, it is a collective summary of the events in Genesis chapter two. It gives us the details and covers all that is created, and summarizes man, his positioning, and the positioning of mankind. (Genesis 2:1-25) gives us a detailed account of God's vision and purpose for handcrafting man, the beginning of mankind, and further builds on (Genesis 1:26).

Genesis chapters 1 and 2 collectively gives us God's blueprint of Adam (man), his identity (God makes man in His image and likeness), purpose, the godly concept of dominion (God puts man in the garden to till and dress it), and man's definition and boundaries (God gives man laws and conditions).

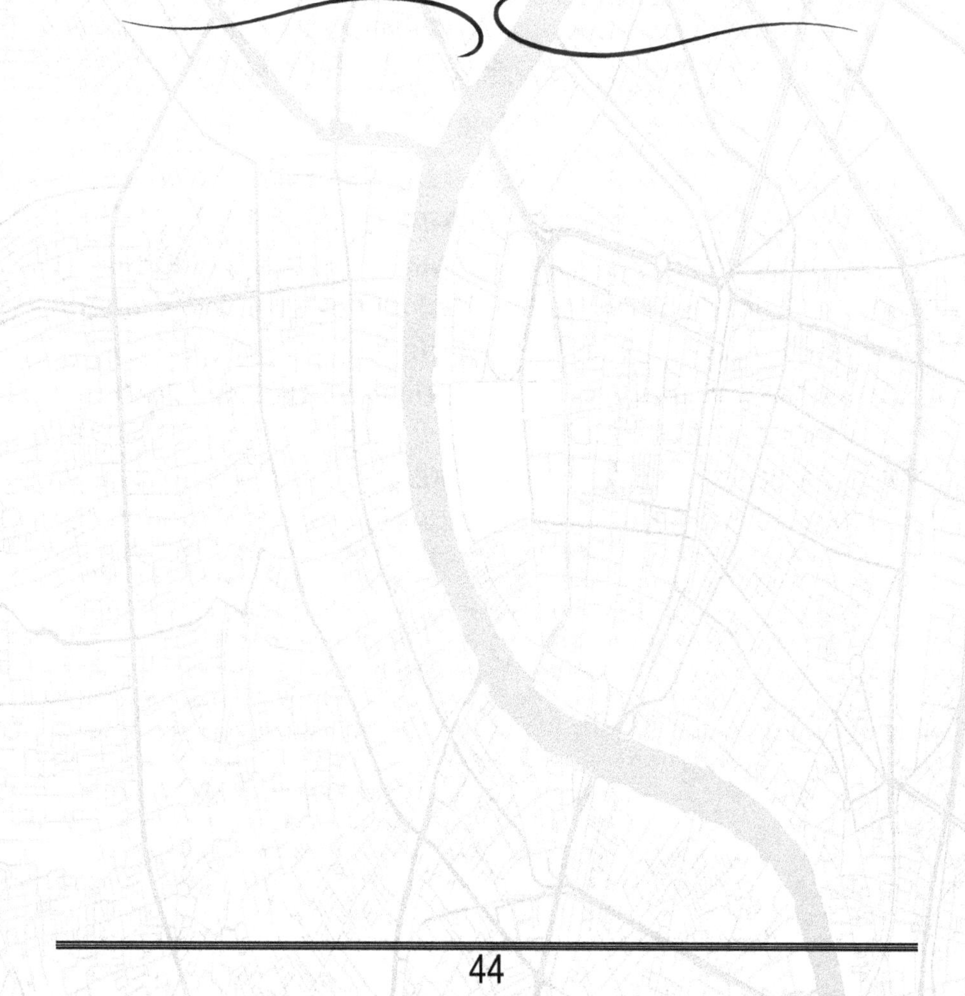

1. Identity: God removed from Adam (that which was taken out of man) woman.
2. Purpose/Need: To fulfill Adam's need: A help meet and companion.
3. Authority & Boundaries: The mother of mankind. To be fruitful and multiply.

Conclusion: Woman was not made with man, but after an unknown period of time when man dwelt alone as the only human on earth, God formed woman from him and presented (gifted) woman to him to assist or help him with his divinely assigned responsibilities, commandments, and to birth humanity.

And the LORD God took the man, and put him into the garden of Eden to dress it and to keep it. And the LORD God commanded the man, saying, Of every tree of the garden thou mayest freely eat: But of the tree of the knowledge of good and evil, thou shalt not eat of it: for in the day that thou eatest thereof thou shalt surely die. And the LORD God said, [It is] not good that the man should be alone; I will make him a help meet for him. (Genesis 2:15-18)

Not of his own, as we would like to believe; but man is under the authority of his Creator. Demonstrating that his authority does not come from within himself, but from what he is entrusted with. The absolute authority has and will always rest with God, creating the only scenario possible: man will always be answerable to God. This represents God's first order, putting Adam in the Garden of Eden where he (man) was to have dominion. With that assigned dominion came responsibility and personal discipline. In positioning Adam in the Garden, God supplied him with everything he needed, and tested his obedience, reverence, and character with what seemed to be a simple challenge of divine boundaries.

Of every tree of the garden you may freely eat; but of the tree of the knowledge of good and evil, thou shall not eat of it: (Genesis 2:16b-17a)

Of all that God created, man is the only one that required testing. The God-like creature who can reason and make choices had to show the Creator that he would choose obedience over self-gratification.

AND OUT OF THE GROUND, THE LORD GOD FORMED EVERY BEAST OF THE FIELD, AND EVERY FOWL OF THE AIR; AND BROUGHT THEM UNTO ADAM TO SEE WHAT HE WOULD CALL THEM: AND WHATSOEVER ADAM CALLED EVERY LIVING CREATURE, THAT WAS THE NAME THEREOF. AND ADAM GAVE NAMES TO ALL CATTLE, AND TO THE FOWL OF THE AIR, AND TO EVERY BEAST OF THE FIELD; BUT FOR ADAM THERE WAS NOT FOUND A HELP MEET FOR HIM. (GENESIS 2:19-20)

A second look at (Genesis 1:20-25) reveals how all living creatures made by God were not only given lane definitions and right-of-ways, but were made after their kind, male and female, and further commanded to be fruitful and multiply. Nature is evidence of their pairing, male and female, as they have remained throughout the ages. However, Adam, out of all God created, is alone. He was formed alone, and until this point, remains alone.

Adam did not receive his helpmeet, although we know he was created with seed and the ability to reproduce, until he recognized there was no suitable mate among creation sufficient for him. Note: there is no evidence of Adam going through a surgery to prepare him to reproduce.

Eve was taken from Adam and formed into a woman because there was an obvious need for him to have a mate, someone created with his needs in mind. Solidifying that all else is unsuitable and off-limits. Out of the love, recognition, compassion, and His own good pleasure, and according to His divine plan, God was moved to make for Adam that which suited Adam, his purpose, and/or boundaries/lanes. Woman is made in the image of Adam, as Adam is made in the image of God, thereby bearing God's likeness.

AND THE LORD GOD CAUSED A DEEP SLEEP TO FALL UPON ADAM, AND HE SLEPT: AND HE TOOK ONE OF HIS RIBS AND CLOSED UP THE FLESH INSTEAD THEREOF; AND THE RIB, WHICH THE LORD GOD HAD TAKEN FROM MAN, MADE HE A WOMAN, AND BROUGHT HER UNTO THE MAN. (GENESIS 2:21-22)

As we recognize, all living creatures, male and female, were called into creation before God created Adam. From this, we can deduce the forming of Eve was not an afterthought by God, but was made manifest, filled in the fullness of time, as the need became evident. Further, that which God made for Adam, he took from Adam's being, signifying that she is in the forethought, plan, and purpose of God. She was already there; simply not yet fashioned apart from Adam. Case in point, Jesus came in the fullness of time, as it became evident there was not an earthly creature who could redeem man. First, the need was clearly identified, and then the manifestation of what was prepared before the foundation of the world was made in the fullness of time, according to the good pleasure of the Creator, to meet the need. As there are many examples in scripture, including Mary, the earthly mother of Jesus the Christ, had been assigned, appointed, and found favor with God to deliver on earth "The Emmanuel: God with us man-child." Which could not take place until the fullness of God's calendar came into existence.

As Adam realized a need for someone like him, God took from him a rib to fashion for him a help meet, "...flesh of Adam's flesh, and bone of Adam's bone." In the same way, Adam is made in the likeness of God, woman is made in the image of Adam, and because she is taken from Adam's being, she will always be part of him. She cannot then, nor now, be taken for granted, be unappreciated, not thought of, nor looked upon as just another of God's living creatures. As the Creator presents her to Adam, he revels in the flesh formed entirely for him. She is not merely made, but designed, not simply designed, but fashioned, not only fashioned, but delivered to him, not simply brought to him, but given to him as a helper to help him in his daily existence and in the fulfillment of the plan and order of God. Unbeknownst to her, she is longed for, needed, and missed! In fulfilling Adam's need, the two are charged, as a couple, as all of creation, to, "be fruitful and multiply." As God presented creation to Adam, he could now, with the pride of all his acquired knowledge, show woman. She is the pride of his life and the treasure of his heart. From their connection, no matter where she is, she will always be close to him and be protected by him. Just as man is to God, this woman is to man.

God is the provider and supplier of all our needs. God knows what we need before we verbalize it. We go looking for what we need outside our boundaries, pressing our way, unaware that we have already been given what we need, manifested or unmanifested, and too often, we negate the blessings on the way.

Unfortunately for many of us, God is the last place we look to have our needs met. We humans often reject or abandon the prescribed course, seeking answers that take us outside our lane, preventing us from naturally inheriting what God has ordained for us to meet our needs. Staying in our lane requires humility and rejecting the following of our personal ego's for self-promotion. We lack the complete understanding that because God is our maker; He knows what we need, and in the fullness of time, will supply our needs. The problem occurs when we step outside the will of God and go on our own without consideration or expectation of the provisions already in God's vision of us: violating the divine order for our lives, while intruding into the lanes of others, unintentionally.

"It is not good that man should be alone."

The great love and respect God has for man is unmistakable in the gifting of woman to man. A gift whose purpose is to assist man in the completion of his assignment, live out his purpose, and honor his God-given lane and boundaries.

"...WHEN I WOULD DO GOOD, EVIL IS PRESENT WITH ME." (ROMANS 7:21)

As evidenced in all creation, wherever there is good, in equal measure, the existence of evil is present.

"...YOU WERE IN EDEN, THE GARDEN OF GOD; EVERY PRECIOUS STONE WAS YOUR COVERING... YOU WERE THE ANOINTED CHERUB WHO COVERS AND PROTECTS, AND I PLACED YOU THERE. YOU WERE ON THE HOLY MOUNTAIN OF GOD; YOU WALKED IN THE MIDST OF THE STONES OF FIRE. YOU WERE BLAMELESS IN YOUR WAYS FROM THE DAY YOU WERE CREATED UNTIL UNRIGHTEOUSNESS WAS FOUND IN YOU. BY THE ABUNDANCE OF YOUR TRADE, YOU WERE INTERNALLY FILLED WITH VIOLENCE, AND YOU SINNED; THEREFORE, I HAVE CAST YOU AS PROFANE FROM THE MOUNTAIN OF GOD. AND I HAVE DESTROYED YOU, O COVERING CHERUB, FROM THE MIDST OF THE STONES OF FIRE. YOUR HEART WAS LIFTED UP BECAUSE OF YOUR BEAUTY; YOU CORRUPTED YOUR WISDOM BY REASON OF YOUR SPLENDOR. I CAST YOU TO THE GROUND; I PUT YOU BEFORE KINGS, THAT THEY MAY SEE YOU..." (EZEKIEL 28:11-19 AMP)

"HOW ART THOU FALLEN FROM HEAVEN, O LUCIFER, SON OF THE MORNING! HOW ART THOU CUT DOWN TO THE GROUND, WHICH DIDST WEAKEN THE NATIONS! FOR THOU HAST SAID IN THINE HEART, I WILL ASCEND INTO HEAVEN, I WILL EXALT MY THRONE ABOVE THE STARS OF GOD: I WILL ASCEND ABOVE THE HEIGHTS OF THE CLOUDS; I WILL BE LIKE THE MOST HIGH..." (ISAIAH 14:12-16)

AND HE SAID UNTO THEM, "I BEHELD SATAN AS LIGHTNING FALL FROM HEAVEN." (LUKE 10:18)

We understand from the scripture references above that there was an existing Creation (Order) in the cosmos before God recreated the present universe as we know it. In that government, God created a being named "Lucifer." He is the bright star referred to as a, "covering cherub." His beauty and magnificence of his abilities caused him to believe he could not only be like God, but he could raise himself above God. The scriptures tell us he was defeated in his attempt to storm heaven, and along with the angels that took part in his rebellion, were cast down into outer darkness. The domain where he existed was called out of existence, leaving a void and chaos in its wake, beneath the heavens.

Lucifer himself was displaced and sentenced to a day of judgment yet to come. He was present as God recreated (replenished) what previously was destroyed. It was against this backdrop Lucifer watched as God created light and called it to overcome darkness, separated the waters from the water, and caused the dry land to appear. We can only imagine the contempt Lucifer experienced as God breathed into this lump of clay; He called man, the breath of life giving him dominion over this new creation. As Adam went about naming the plants and animals and exploring the trees, there was an adversary watching and waiting for an opportunity to trip him up and deny God the praise and glory of this new creature and creation.

That adversarial presence is present in our dominion, as he was in the dominion he was expelled from. As he awaits his final judgment, he still has the same agenda; to steal what has been given to man and kill the glory that is due to the Creator. He is known by many names, including Satan, The Devil, The Adversary, and/or the Evil One. He lives to derail man and all mankind, so that we too might be damned, and share in the eternal punishment awaiting him. To do so, he must provoke God into carrying out His own decree and judgment against man for violating His commandments,

In the day that thou eatest thereof thou shalt surely die..." (Genesis 2:17), causing man to miss eternal life. ("Such is the confidence we have toward God through Christ." 2 Corinthians 3:4). Satan's greatest weapon is our ignorance of his devices and the subtleness of his approach.

Yet he, this anti-God, anti-man spirit being, is traveling to and from, up and down throughout the earth, seeking whom he may devour. For he has but one purpose that is to steal, kill and destroy. (Job 1:6-7, 1 Peter 5:8, John 10:10).

Now the serpent was more subtile than any beast of the field which the Lord God had made. (Genesis 3:1a).

He approached not the man to whom God had given the law of commandments; but he approached the woman who had received the commandments second-hand. The weight of the commandment rested not on her, but on the man whom God personally gave the commandment. Therefore, she carried not the consciousness of obedience or disobedience that Adam felt. The test itself was evidence man had within him the ability to make the wrong decision. As God knew this, so did Lucifer. Adam wanted to take from the tree, but out of fear and respect, touched it not. Satan needed a means to get the forbidden fruit into Adam's hands. This newcomer, Eve, provided the perfect vehicle. Lucifer, with the subtlety of a wise and trusted friend, approached Eve disguised as a serpent. From the ease of their encounter, we can deduce this was not the first time the serpent had spoken to Eve. But over time, had open dialog with Eve. His knowledge and wisdom opened the way for trust and confidentiality. She took of the forbidden fruit, and invited Adam to eat with her, trespassing the commandment of God. Mission accomplished! Both Adam and Eve went outside their God-appointed and defined lane, overstepped their God-appointed boundaries, and brought upon themselves poverty and the curse of death. (Initiating the requirement of man's blood, for life is in the blood.)

Adam exercised his dominion over everything God brought before him; but over himself he failed the test. He could have had everything in the Garden, except for one thing. The one thing that brought about disobedience. Adam lost the only thing created in the image and likeness of God: eternal life. Despite Adam's disobedience and sin, God had and still has a covenant relationship with man. Rather than canceling His relationship with man, He modified it by placing additional boundaries on man's freedom and liberty. Adam's disobedience led to his removal from the Garden and restricted him from the Tree of Life. However, our covenant-keeping God provided a way for man's eventual salvation and eternal life.

For God commanded his love toward us, in that, while we were yet sinners, Christ died for us. (Romans 5:8)

Wherefore, by one man sin entered into the world, and death by sin: and so death passed upon all men, for all have sinned. (Romans 5:12)

Nevertheless, death reigned from Adam to Moses, even over them that had not sinned after the similitude of Adam's transgression, who is the figure of him that was to come. (Romans 5:14)

The headship and dominion that rested with man was still exclusively his. However, his lane now took on new dimensions, boundaries, and further definition.

We may question why an all-knowing, ever-present God would have to ask “Adam, where are you?” Adam’s hiding himself from God was in fact evidence Adam had eaten from the forbidden tree of the Knowledge of Good and Evil. Yet God came to where Adam was, not to condemn him as Adam proposed, but to confront him, whom He loved. Adam was in fear of the pending judgment for his disobedience, reasoned in himself he needed to hide from the presence of God. This is the plight of many men today. They seek to avoid God’s presence from their disobedience. They did not know of God’s arms of grace and mercy; that despite our shortcomings, it was then, and is still today, the safest hiding place available to man. God was with Adam as He is with us today; constant and consistently seeking the redemption and restoration of man and mankind. His tender voice of compassion draws near to us that we might cry out to Him who is our ever-present help. “Here I am Lord!” This is our lane!

Adam offered God an excuse he expected would shift the burden of his disobedience away from him to his mate, Eve. However, "The woman you gave me..." excuse further convicted him. Adam was, in fact, responsible for his actions and that of Eve. He not only had dominion over the Garden, but headship over all God had entrusted him with, and that included the woman God gave to him.

Eve, this wide-eyed newcomer, beguiled by Lucifer, was in her inner being convinced what she heard from the serpent was true. The serpent brought her to the point of questioning God's motives. She believed that by eating the forbidden fruit, she would be wise. So, she took the forbidden fruit from the tree (that Adam could not do morally), ate it, and, "...gave also unto her husband with her; and he did eat."

Unknowingly, she acted as a free agent without allegiances to either. Unknowingly, she created a chasm between God and Adam. The thing Lucifer, man's adversarial force, had plotted to do from the beginning. Eve's actions and her influence overshadowed Adam's conscience of obedience, which gave him permission to make a choice to disobey God's commandments and eat the forbidden fruit. As we can conclude from God's creative pattern, this was just the opposite of what was expected. It was Adam who was to influence Eve, and she was to be subject to his leadership. Eve's actions were out-of-order and beyond her prescribed lane. Whether intentionally or unintentionally, she opened the doorway to both sin and systematic human perversion.

According to Webster's Dictionary, perversion is the alteration of something from its original course, meaning, or state, to a distortion or corruption of what was first intended.

If we follow the scripture verses that refer to the works of the fallen angel, Lucifer, better known as Satan, the adversary of God and man, we know he is the author of perversion. It was the works of perversion that were first found in him. God created him as the covering cherubim of the mount of God. He was the chief musician, the most beautiful angel, and had in his treasury every precious and beautiful stone. He was perfect in all his ways until iniquity (perversion) was found in him. It is in his rebellion that he seeks to destroy everything God has made or ordained as good, beautiful, and all that would bless man and bring glory to God through man. Lucifer's interaction with Eve was the first of many deceptive tricks he used to discredit the crowning work of God's creation to distract man from his calling, position, and lane.

Being expelled from the Garden, which God planted just for him to dress and keep, forced man to toil (work) the land outside the Garden to sustain himself and his family. Dominance was no longer a simple blessing, but now a responsibility and the ultimate means of survival. He was no longer solely a caretaker, but now a laborer. Adam's life depended on him laboring for his food. This is a consequence of Adam's failure when tested. His disobedience led to him being a failed recipient of all God created for him. He had been silent when he should have stood up for his responsibility to take charge and defend what he knew was right in the face of wrong. Adam being made in the image of God (to imitate God) did not strengthen his resolve to be obedient to the directives of God. He yielded the entrusted estate of mankind to Lucifer, the enemy of man and God.

If there is a true and concurrent accusation of man's shortcomings, today it is that man's failure to be obedient, in the Garden and to the directives of God, has yielded the entrusted society and social order into the hands of the enemy. Man must realize his authority, as is God's authority, is not always recognized as, "the Authority," and, therefore, his position (right standings) will not resound favorably when it comes to the desires of others having yielded to natural influences, emotions, and/or prideful and lustful actions. Even with the love, grace, and mercy of God, there are consequences for disobedience and other boundaries of restriction.

Without biblical knowledge and instructions that come with the awareness of pre-determined order and assignments, one is left to determine an order for themselves. In the free and equal society in which we live, every man, woman, boy or girl is doing whatever is right in their own eyes. Leaving little room for order or respect. In this so-called liberated society, there is little or no consideration for lanes or boundaries for personal and/or societal restrictions. This mind of liberation (free agency) allows for the perpetuation of the spirit of, "whatever," in the minds and souls of each generation. The void of biblical knowledge and authority in our society opens the doorways for each of us to be elevated to a status of person-hood equality. Wherein we trample over what man's Creator had established to exercise the assumed rights under no authority. This mindset elevates each of us to our own authority, while breeding chaos, disharmony, and heightening disrespect.

In this new twenty-first century age, there is disharmony and competition throughout our society, and especially in our homes. Many times, the man is unprepared to lead, out/over talked, and disrespected. The woman cannot find a mate prepared to be a husband (educated, trained, and self-disciplined to be the provider of protection, security, and stability), and is becoming a power of one. If the feminist motto is true, women live and define their existence by one fundamental truth, "by me, for me, and controlled by me." Resulting in the change of distinct roles where men were the breadwinners of old, and the job assignments once solidly occupied by males are now filled by both males and females. Financial opportunities have increased for females who once had limited job choices and sources of income, even though they remain unequal to their male counterparts. Thereby, creating a twenty-first century female who has become self-sufficient and responsible for fulfilling her own need to thrive. A reality where the woman competes educationally and intelligently with her male counterparts as they apply for the same scholarships and advancements.

Women earnestly apply themselves to accomplish the task at hand more often than men. While men appear more selective with what they devote themselves to. Undoubtedly, women are more family-oriented than men, having birthed the children who must be cared for, fed, and educated. Today's woman, with her financial abilities and accomplishments, resembles the (Proverbs 31) Woman. However, even with those exceptional qualities, she may have the propensity to get drunk on herself, her self-worth, and her personal accomplishments. The Biblical (Proverbs 31)

Woman honors her husband and is praised by him. However, in today's society, his praise may not be enough. Men must be prepared for leadership, which includes him being educated and/or acquiring the skills that produce an income sufficient to support a marriage and a family. Men who are not prepared to take their rightful place as the leader in his home may find themselves overruled and/or not needed.

Too many times, man has found himself unable to stabilize a marriage or find fulfillment in their marriage or potential marriage relationship. They have stepped outside the boundaries of their lane and left their responsibilities for the woman to fulfill. His absence and/or lack of commitment is regarded as his refusal to commit to his role as the head of the household and the covering for his family. Often the wife is forced to find additional employment or sign up for welfare to provide for the family. Women have increasingly become the breadwinners and head of household as single parents due to the man's failure to operate in his assigned lane.

This has forced women to get caught up in the cycle as strong and independent women who raise their children alone. Many women now freely stepping into a lane that was not their own because she was raised without a father figure or a male covering in her youth. In the same vein, males who have grown up in a single-parent home with a strong, independent woman as the head of the household do not have the capacity to operate from the father-head of household model. Therefore, they expect (which is against their own nature) the woman to occupy the leadership role and be the authority in their relationships. The third scenario in the mismatch relationship concept is present in marriage where the husband or wife knows the role or the lane in which God has ordained for them, and the other mate does not have a clue nor is respectful of the other's expectations.

If we can get out of our own way and/or our need to have our assumed rights realized, we can look at the pattern of order/lanes set before us in the Godhead. When God said, "Let us make man...," it was to Jesus (His Son) and to the Holy Spirit that He spoke (Genesis 1:26). The Bible further says that in God there is order and discipline: a pre-defined, God-given, and recognized lane of service and operation. In this relationship, we recognize Jesus, the Word, speaks all things into existence; and fulfills the scripture that says, "All things were made by Him, and without Him was not anything made that was made..." When God said, "Let us make man...," it was to Jesus (His Son) and to the Holy Spirit (His Spirit) that He spoke in (Genesis 1:26). That divine order and discipline speaks to the divine design, ordained lanes, and creation's mode of operation, while admonishing us to follow His divine pattern and plan of humility.

Let this mind be in you, which was also in Christ Jesus: Who, being in the form of God, thought it not robbery to be equal with God: But made himself of no reputation, and took upon him the form of a servant, and was made in the likeness of men: And being found in fashion as a man, he humbled himself, and became obedient unto death, even the death of the cross. Wherefore God also hath highly exalted him, and given him a name which is above every name: (Philippians 2:5-9)

Humility is a venture God abundantly rewards.

It does not matter what earthly titles or achievements a person might have; there are gender assignments. These assignments have nothing to do with who is the smartest, the brightest, or the quickest, who made better grades, who can boast about their scholastic achievements, or who makes the most money; nor is it about the one who is the most articulate. It is not even about the one automatically entitled to be the spokesperson for the family or occupy the coveted role of leadership.

"For as we have many members in one body, and all members have not the same office." (function) (Romans 12:4)

In the same way, there are physical attributes that set us apart as male and female. There are both genetic and physiological markings that innately mark our gender assignment. Boys are not called boys solely because they run, jump, climb, explore, or tinker with nature. Girls are not called girls because they play with dolls, hang around mom, and have a propensity towards neatness and cleanliness. Regardless of the gender assignment, either can be trained or adapt to any of the activities previously mentioned. These characteristics are NOT indicators of gender orientation; they are merely evidence of environmental adaptations.

However, there are, with or without gender influences, strong indicators like physical and sexual preparations clearly evident in the womb and in the fullness of time that speak to one's inner code assignment. Along with the natural, these assignments come with psychological coding that makes each gender fulfilled or unfulfilled, known as gender lanes. Man, in his natural state, and without perversion, will seek and aspire to the position of leadership, headship, dominion, and/or control. It is not simply a societal appointment; he is genetically predestined for his role as leader, provider, protector, and priest of his home. This includes him as the spokesperson and watcher of potential enemies that would interfere with his domain or violate those with whom he is in a relationship with and charged to defend. What he needs and demands foremost from his mate is respect, honor, and reverence. This is key in any relationship, whether he is consciously aware of his responsibilities or not.

How is the woman to respect, honor, and treat the man during the development of their marriage relationship? Respectfully and graciously, she places the man on the throne in his home and watches him develop into the husband, father, defender, provider, etc. he is divinely assigned to be. The woman offers him the opportunity to bring home the bacon (even if it was purchased from her account), and showers him with love and adoration (to teach him how to do the same for her). She continuously encourages him to step into his role as the leader of the family, while keeping watch to know when he needs help. She is attentive in learning the specifics of his accepted ways of receiving her help. It is through the woman's actions and treatment of him that she encourages him to be the man of their together-build home. Her encouragement gives him permission to show up as the parent and father who spends quality time with their children. Her smile lights up his heart and shows she is listening to and interested in not only hearing what he is saying, but in understanding him.

As she gazes searchingly into his eyes, when he is struggling, she learns what is troubling him without him ever having to say a word. During their various conversations, she gives him the same undivided attention she desires. She uses any excuse to find time to snuggle with him and to solicit his input on pressing and/or upcoming family matters and her personal decisions. She talks lovingly to him with her eyes and watches him shine and flex his manly muscles as he comfortably leans back, crosses his legs, and laces his hands behind his head in satisfaction with his life and his marriage!

"...Wives reverence your husbands." (Ephesians 5:33)

Disrespecting and/or dishonoring him, bad-mouthing him to others, and/or cursing him to his face or behind his back, are deal-breakers that will send the man's soul searching for another home.

Although man can accept subordination to another man, he will seek to find ways to chart his own course. Even though times have changed, and women have the opportunity to become educated and prove themselves, men will consider it unnatural to be under the authority of a woman and question her ability to be an effective leader and decision-maker. As is expected, many will find it difficult to accept and understand this behavior and/or mindset. However, it is not until we understand the fact that man is made in the image and likeness of God, given the charge to exercise dominion, and is expected to be glorified as the lord in his home and/or field of labor, that this behavior or mindset will be accepted and/or tolerated.

Likewise, we must relate back to creation to find what is the innate code and reason for the disposition of the woman both then and now.

As we will recall, Lucifer (referred to as Satan) was deported from the upper heavens and forced to abide in the lower stratosphere by God. As Lucifer watches, God moves on the face of the deep void and begins to create. In jealousy, Lucifer watches God crown His new creation as He toils over a dirt creature called man and breathes Himself into the creature made in His image and likeness. To add insult to injury, God forms a covenant relationship between Himself and man, and gives him dominion over all that previously had been dominated by Lucifer.

Lucifer, a God created being who lost his domain, was cast out of heaven to await his final judgment, is now forced to regard himself as inferior to man, and is resentful of the authority that now rests in the hands of man. It was upon this stage, that Eve was shaped from the bone of man, fashioned, and presented to Adam (man).

AND THE LORD GOD SAID "...IT IS NOT GOOD THAT MAN SHOULD BE ALONE. I WILL MAKE HIM A HELP MEET FOR HIM... AND THE LORD GOD CAUSED A DEEP SLEEP TO FALL UPON ADAM, AND HE SLEPT: AND HE TOOK ONE OF HIS RIBS AND CLOSED UP THE FLESH INSTEAD THEREOF; AND THE RIB, WHICH THE LORD GOD HAD TAKEN FROM MAN, MADE HE A WOMAN, AND BROUGHT HER UNTO THE MAN." (GENESIS 2:18,21-22)

We can imagine Eve must have clung to Adam, as he is the only being that resembles her. The trust she has with Adam and God is automatic, which stands to reason why she would freely hear and receive this other creature's influence as truthful and trustworthy. With his subtlety, trickery, and wisdom, the serpent moves to destroy her innocence and open her eyes to the inside information that better explains what Adam told her. Should she have questioned God's motive for keeping this inside information from Adam? Should she consult God with the inside information the serpent gave her before acting on it? Why should this trusted creature, the serpent, lie to her? Surely Adam had told her of God's commandments; but why should she not see the serpent as a trustworthy advisor, especially if what he said will make her wise?

Surely, she had created a respectful and trustworthy relationship with Adam, in whom she saw herself. As the scriptures state, Eve came on the scene to be a help meet, a companion for Adam, and as such, Eve is not a covenant-holder in the covenant relationship between God and Adam. The covenant guidelines she received were shared as second-hand information from Adam. When Eve acted upon the inside information she received from the serpent, Adam's authority over her had not been established nor verbally declared.

Where is the evidence of Eve's relationship with God? Before Eve's arrival in the garden, when God came walking in the Garden, He called out to Adam as he has dominion over all creation. After Eve is created and presented to Adam, he became responsible for her and everything she did. Although Eve was with Adam when he communed with God, she was basically eavesdropping on their daily conversations and interactions.

When Eve is presented to Adam, there are three influences present in the Garden, with each having their own expectations of the woman, Eve.

God's expectations:

From scripture, we can conclude Eve was created as a help meet and companion to the man, Adam. God gave her to him as his wife to be fruitful and multiply. She is to be the mother of all mankind/humanity. Even here, we can trace the creative footprint of God and the lane assignment of Eve.

And God blessed them, and God said unto them, Be fruitful, and multiply, and replenish the earth, and subdue it: and have dominion over the fish of the sea, and over the fowl of the air, and over every living thing that moveth upon the earth. (Genesis 1:28)

Need:	Adam's wife and the mother of mankind.
Purpose:	A mate fitted for Adam, the genetic opposite of Adam.
Definition:	Called woman, Adam's help meet.

Boundaries: To be subject to God's commandments through Adam.

UNTO THE WOMAN HE SAID, I WILL GREATLY MULTIPLY THY SORROW AND THY CONCEPTION: IN SORROW THOU SHALT BRING FORTH CHILDREN; AND THY DESIRE SHALL BE TO THY HUSBAND, AND HE SHALL RULE OVER THEE. (GENESIS 3:16)

Man's expectations:

Eve is to accompany him, admire him, learn from him, and eventually become the mother of mankind/humanity. (Genesis 2:18, 23; 3:16)

More than a dream come true, she was the custom-made answer to his need, and the most beautiful creature his eyes had ever beheld. Surely his heart must have gone out totally and completely for her. As his mate, she was to accompany him as he dressed and kept the Garden. She is the weaker vessel, given to respect his position, his authority, and his dominion, and to be one with him as his wife. (Genesis 2:22-24)

Lucifer's view of her:

Eve was a newcomer, a learner, gullible, innocent, teachable, approachable, and persuasively vulnerable. She is the naive vessel Lucifer plans to use to derail God's plan for mankind. She was perfect for his plans. Eve was open-minded enough for him to run his game on her. He knew his wisdom, intelligence, and/or cunningness were no match for her knowledge, emotions, or experience. (Genesis 3:4)

Lucifer, through the eyes of the serpent, watched Eve's interactions with Adam and understood the influence she had over him. She represented the perfect means for him to tempt man and derail God's plan for mankind.

The woman, the newcomer, was limited in her wisdom and knowledge. Her assignment, spoken or unspoken, was to watch, listen, learn, and help whenever necessary. One would reason that she possibly knew only what Adam told or showed her. As the newcomer, it is understandable that her knowledge of what was happening behind the scenes and/or outside of man's relationship with God is extremely limited. So where did she fit? A creature of intelligence like Adam, with a free will, capable of thinking for herself. She is the offspring of the Creator God and Adam. God took the rib from Adam and fashioned her into a human being. What was she to do or think? Apart from Adam, she had developed a trusting ear to what was already present in the Garden, and who manifested himself as a serpent. Surely our biblical record of this climatic event was not her first encounter with Lucifer, so cunningly disguised as a serpent with a smooth, welcoming, and soothing voice. Over time, he won both her trust and her ear, into which he now sought to impart perverted reasoning and rationale to her human-thinking. He knew it would condemn the posterity of man. When she heard enough from this being hiding within the serpent, she made what appeared to her as a reasonable decision.

Eve, like so many of us, is born into a world of which she knew nothing about. We can only reason with our natural minds and see with our natural eyes. Therefore, our influences appeal to us by our natural abilities to accept or reject whatever has been introduced to us. The natural thinking is the ready-lens through which we can reason, judge, and make decisions. We are not aware of what is good for us or why there should be a supreme being in whom we have limited knowledge, and no visual image of either. Who is to govern us, decide for us, and/or set the path in which we should follow? As infants and adolescents, we are not aware that there is an enemy who, from personal experience, understands our human desires for self-gratification, self-control, and the ability to determine and exercise our own free will. It is this enemy's plot, as it was with Eve, to take advantage of our naivety and capitalize on our vulnerability. He will always show us a way to self-glory and personal authority in which we can exercise our free-will. He will present us with a way that seems right to us, knowing that therein lies the way to destruction.

Women must always be on guard. There is within them an unspoken inferiority complex born out of placement and ranking next to men. Her desire is not only to her husband, but a resentment to the placement of his authority. Women will always aspire to be in a position of greater self-worth, as it relates to their ranking and comparison to males, and in their personal achievements; both with and apart from a man. Women both accept and reject the assigned role as mother, wife, and homemaker, while cherishing the fact that only a woman can bring forth life and cause a man to experience great pleasure and joy. A woman's attraction, looks, and appearance can be both to her benefit and her demise. She is a competitive contender in all she finds is a worthy cause. Depending on the seasons of life, she may experience any or all these conditions.

As mentioned above, she may desire choices and decisions that chart a path of her own choosing. However, the woman who accepts the assignment of her lane as a divinely appointed lane assignment finds great contentment and focus as she works through each day. It was by Eve's hands that the vehicle to Adam's trespass was provided.

"...She took of the fruit thereof, and did eat, and gave also unto her husband with her: and he did eat." (Genesis 3:6)

It was not until after the fall that Eve received recognition from Adam that solidified her identity and her position in his life. "The woman whom thou gave to be with me..." (Genesis 3:12)

Without understanding its significance, Eve acted outside the expected order of creation. Some perceive Eve made her presence known, even though Lucifer had used her to create dissention between God and man. Her influence gave Adam the boldness and gumption he used to disobey God and disregard His commandments. Solidifying the woman's role in the man's life forever. We can only wonder if Adam ever considered how his actions would have long-lasting consequences, and in some cases, have become the generational curses humanity is still struggling with today?

The influence and positioning of this creature called, "woman."

Unto the woman He said, I will greatly multiply thy sorrow and thy conception; in sorrow thou shalt bring forth children; and thy desire shall be to thy husband, and he

SHALL RULE OVER THEE. (GENESIS 3:16)

God's declaration into and over the woman's life then is still her assigned lane today. She is to assist man in his assignments, attend to his comfort, be the mother and caregiver of his children, and share all that he provides. In punishment for her unwillingness to keep the commandments as told by Adam, and for influencing her husband to step outside the confines of his covenant relationship with God, the woman will continuously be regarded as the weaker being, needing the man's covering for protection and provision, and be subject to his leadership. This suggests the woman's role centers around that of her husband and childbearing. Modern women strongly suggest the assigned lane, as it was stated then, is outdated, prehistorical, and antiquated.

Therefore, the consensus is that the original lane assignment does not apply to today's woman. Especially since women have proven themselves capable of multitasking and managing a multi-faceted agenda. Yet the truth about assigned lanes is that they do not change simply because the circumstances in life have changed. Many women are multitasking because the male is out of place or missing for whatever reason. It may be because the man deserted his God ordained assigned lane because he lacks the knowledge base to know what it looks like to be a father, provider, and head of his household. Whether anyone ever taught the man his lane assignments and boundaries, his innate or genetic disposition informs him of the dominion God gave man in the Garden over all creation.

In the same way, Eve, the woman, is innately or genetically reminded daily as to her assigned lane and/or role from what God declared would occur in her life when He said:

"... I will greatly multiply thy sorrow and thy conception; in sorrow thou shalt bring forth children; and thy desire shall be to thy husband, and he shall rule over thee." (Genesis 3:16)

Therefore, where there is a void in the family unit, many believe it to be a direct result of an irresponsible, unemployed, and/or underemployed man. In either case, many men have been displaced or denied their role as the head of the family and its provider. Before we can close our case folder, we must also consider that many women enter the workforce voluntarily, which has no bearing on the man's presence or ability to provide. Education, job availability and/or the current living standards have demanded more women enter the workforce. This demand is further driven by an inner need for personal achievement and advancement, which offers the woman the opportunity to be much more than a homemaker. She now can become a successful professional woman who is sought after, respected, and admired. Therefore, the assigned lanes for the man and woman become a challenge to maintain, while bringing forth another level of fulfillment and in producing an income that provides a greater standard of living than the male's income alone, which supports the commonality of two-income households.

This in no way negates gender-lane assignments, but often

creates a void in the family's time together and in child rearing. In return, it requires greater cooperation and sharing of previously assigned gender lane assignments. As is both expected and evident, these arrangements will continue to increase individual stress levels as each family member struggles to have their needs met.

Many believe it is optional for women to have a husband and/or a man to have a wife. However, according to scripture, man and woman must marry, be fruitful and multiply (bring forth children), and that the man is to be the head of his wife (the woman). His assignment includes providing not only for his family, but as the leader of both his family and the community he resides within. In the absence of the committed male who is conscious of his role and God assigned lane, many women have had no choice but to step up and be independent. Which has blurred the assigned gender roles and created a necessity for women to be self-sufficient and the head of the household. The women who have taken on the responsibility of being the head of their household struggle to fulfill the assigned lane responsibilities for both the male and the female. This often brings on a level of stress that greatly limits the woman's ability to function as expected and live a fulfilled life.

In her book, "Molly Bawn (1878)," Margaret Wolfe Hungerford wrote "...beauty, is in the eye of the beholder..." Which is exactly what occurred in (Genesis 6:1-2), "And it came to pass, when men began to multiply on the face of the earth, and daughters were born unto them, that the sons of God saw the daughters of men that they were fair; and they took them wives of all which they chose." (Jude 6) further explains who the sons of God are when it says, "And the angels which kept not their first estate, but left their own habitation, he hath reserved in everlasting chains under darkness unto the judgment of the great day." It is easy to see the similarity in how men acted in Bible days and how they behave today. In both cases, we can find instances where every man did what was right in his own eyes. The wickedness ("And God saw that the wickedness of man was great in the earth and that every imagination of the thought of man's heart was only evil continually." (Genesis 6:5) God speaks of in Genesis 6:5 is a continuation of Lucifer's original plan to destroy the relationship between God and His created man.

As we delve further into the lanes' assignments, we can identify two conditions that can be traced back to Lucifer's interference in the relationship between God and man and his influence, as the serpent he had over the woman. Just as the woman saw the fruit was pleasant to the eyes, and good to eat, she ate thereof. This represents the actions and choices of the Sons of God in their fallen state. "...the Sons of God, saw the daughters of men that they were fair and took them wives of all they had chosen." (Genesis 6:2). To further understand the significance of this event, it is believed the, "Sons of God," are the fallen angels that were kicked out of heaven with Lucifer, and now are imps who took for themselves human bodies to inhabit. It was while in those bodies that they mated with the women they had chosen. Secondly, in (Genesis 6:4), we learn they bore children with the women they chose, who "...became mighty men which were of old, men of renown."

The sons of God failed to adhere to the boundary constraints of their created lanes. This fallen influence not only altered, but perverted man, and as the women bore children unto them, their children became like those that fathered them. It stands to reason, simply because they inhabited human bodies does not mean they left behind the behaviors and actions that led to them being thrown out of Heaven: rebellious, lawless, ungodly, self-gratifying, fallen, and/or corrupt.

The earth also was corrupt before God, and the earth was filled with violence. And God looked upon the earth, and behold, it was corrupt; for all flesh had corrupted his way upon the earth. And God said unto Noah, The end of all flesh is come before me; for the earth is filled with violence through them; and, behold, I will destroy them with the earth. (Genesis 6:11-13)

Here again, we find God's overflowing love and heart of redemption for man.

But Noah found grace in the eyes of the Lord ...Noah was a just man and perfect in his generations, and Noah

WALKED WITH GOD. (GENESIS 6:8,9)

"AND BEHOLD, I, EVEN I, DO BRING A FLOOD OF WATERS UPON THE EARTH, TO DESTROY ALL FLESH, WHEREIN IS THE BREATH OF LIFE, FROM UNDER HEAVEN; AND EVERYTHING THAT IS IN THE EARTH SHALL DIE. BUT WITH THEE WILL I ESTABLISH MY COVENANT; AND THOU SHALT COME INTO THE ARK, THOU, AND THY SONS, AND THY WIFE, AND THY SONS' WIVES WITH THEE. AND OF EVERY LIVING THING OF ALL FLESH, TWO OF EVERY SORT SHALT THOU BRING INTO THE ARK, TO KEEP THEM ALIVE WITH THEE; THEY SHALL BE MALE AND FEMALE." (GENESIS 6:17-19)

AND THE LORD SAID UNTO NOAH, "COME THOU AND ALL THY HOUSE INTO THE ARK; FOR THEE HAVE I SEEN RIGHTEOUS BEFORE ME IN THIS GENERATION." (GENESIS 7:1)

And God caused a great flood to come upon the earth. Read (Genesis 7: 10-24).

It was the faithful service and conduct of Noah that purchased his salvation, and that of his wife, his sons, and their wives. Despite the devastation of the flood, which was meant to wipe out evil, generations later, there are giants in the land. ("...and moreover, we saw the children of Anak there (giants, the sons of Arbo"). (Numbers 13:28)

The book of Jude tells us the angels left, "...kept not their first estate (fallen angels), but left their own habitation, He (God) hath reserved in everlasting chains under darkness unto the judgment of the great day." (Jude 6). Therefore, we can conclude the work of the imps (fallen angels) had polluted mankind and those genetic dispositions lived on in the descendants of Noah, whether from the sons of Noah or the wives of Noah's sons. It is further evidenced in (Jude 7-8),

> ***Even as Sodom and Gomorrah and the cities about them in like manner, given themselves over to fornication, and going after strange flesh are set forth as an example. Likewise, also these filthy dreamers defile the flesh, despise dominion, and speak evil of dignities. (Jude 7-8)***

The Bible reveals to us that these descendants of Noah in early Bible history were ungodly men and women, worshipers of wood, stone, and all types of precious metals; but not the God of creation, for their hearts were far from him, having become, "whatever's," following their imagination without Godly boundaries, discipline, and/or definition.

And God saw the heart of man was continuously wicked and perverse as before the flood. It was out of this condition God found Abraham, and through him promised a people with whom He would later enter a covenant relationship and give them written laws, precepts, and concepts upon which they would follow. It was out of this covenant people; the shadow was given to the Savior Redeemer to come. However, long before that promise was fulfilled, God used the covenant holders to drive out and utterly destroy the sons of Arbo.

Mankind is not only stained with the sins and debt of Adam, for which a blood sacrifice is required, but we all need to be regenerated. In which our minds and hearts must be cleansed and renewed. Expecting that man will turn from the ways of a, "whatever," toward God, our Creator, who made us according to His plan and for His purpose, that humanity will occupy the lanes as prescribed, described, and set forth.

For this cause, God prepared beforehand and provided one remedy: the body and blood sacrifice of the promised lamb, Jesus Christ. This, Our Redeemer, formally introduced in Genesis as the Word of God, born of a woman, having taken on flesh, and walked this earth as a sinless man who would redeem us from the penalty of death, ushering in a new dispensation of grace and spiritual cleansing. The shedding of His blood as the innocent lamb in the Garden to cover Adam's and Eve's nakedness not only paid our blood debt, but also showed us the way to repentance and salvation through faith. Through Him, we are inheritors of the grace of God, which placed the sin of our disobedient waywardness on Him and transferred His righteousness to us. Mankind's redeemed lane is to forsake the perverted ways of our flesh and be followers of Jesus Christ. (Genesis 3:21; John 1: 1-15, Psalms 22, 45, 55; Isaiah 9, 11, 53)

Without biblical knowledge and instructions that come with the awareness of pre-determined order and assignments, one is left to determine an order for themselves. In this free and equal society, each man, woman, boy and/or girl, as before the flood, does what is right in their own eyes, leaving little room for order and/or respect. In this so-called liberated society, there are minor considerations for lanes and/or boundaries, where there are personal and societal restrictions. This mind of liberation or free agency allows the perpetuation of the spirit of whatever in the minds and souls of each generation. This void of Biblical knowledge and authority in our society opens the doorways for each of us to be elevated to a status of person-hood equality, where we trample over what man's creator established to exercise man's assumed rights under no authority. It is this mindset that elevates each of us to our own authority, thus breeding chaos, disharmony, societal decay and heightening the disrespect for God and man.

With all going on in our world today, women are still pushed, pulled, and guided by three forces present in the Garden when she arrived. (Refer to the section on “Woman drawn and driven by three relationships or influences”). Most times today, the woman becomes confused about her place when she is invited and made to feel uninvited. When she is made to feel included and not included simultaneously. For some women, there is no worse position to be in than in the room, but not included in the conversation, listened to, or heard, and when asking for prayer, they are preyed on instead. Many love her, but she seldom feels secure in the love of those closest to her. There are even cases where her beauty is admired, but she is misused, and even abused when the focus is on her physical attributes. Teaching her how to use her beauty and physical attributes to get the attention needed to influence the mind of man is a delicate balancing act. Although this behavior is accepted, sometimes the woman is admonished and rebuked when she is encouraged to follow the dictates of the world. Some would suggest women have gained the freedom to live her life as she chooses and are liberated from the restraints once put on women; yet she is bound by those same ideologies and pressured to remember her place. As is the case today, many women are just as intelligent as any man, but are not viewed, or treated as an equal; nor will they ever obtain equality with the man.

As the woman is created from the emotion God has for man, she is an emotional being who longs to be loved. However, she withdraws for fear of being taken advantage of when she is open and/or vulnerable.

Yes, there is that word again, vulnerable. Being vulnerable is a dreadful place for any woman; one she avoids. It is the place in which she consciously, or often unconsciously, spends her time, mental energy, and reserves. As a little girl, it is the one place she is most haunted, and where she tries to outrun the trailing footsteps she hears in her teens and early adulthood. It is that thing that drives her to be educated, to compete, and to exceed beyond her classmates. The fear of pending vulnerability drives her to get her own things: her own apartment, her own job, her own car, her own gun, etc. Yet when she lays down at night alone in her own bed or snuggles up on her own couch, that knowledge comes rushing in like a feared intruder, "I am vulnerable." Leaving the grocery store at night, parking in a full or empty garage, a walk down a quiet and/or unfamiliar street, moving to a new and/or unfamiliar location, going alone to the restroom in an unfamiliar place, and/or maybe just encountering a stare or glance from an over-admiring male, while fully clothed, but feeling as if he is undressing her with his eyes, all remind her of the vulnerability she despises. For many women, this feeling is unavoidable.

Women have made significant advancements, challenging the male in every endeavor, proving themselves over and over again to be as intelligent, industrious, and savvy as any man. Walking the walk and talking the talk. She can indeed, "bring home the bacon, fry it up in the pan, yet never let a man forget she is a woman." She can argue, curse, fight, buy the pants and wear them, be the head of the household, and the family matriarch. But in the quiet moments and stillness of night, she must again, at some point, come face-to-face with the fact that apart from a loving and caring man in her life... she is vulnerable. In all that she has achieved or how well she can hold it all together, and in doing so, demands respect... she is vulnerable. Often with a sense of being out of place, "questioning her lane," and uncovered. This condition contradicts everything that this new-age woman represents.

The Biblical reference is that men should not be alone. What is unstated, but true, is that neither should women be alone. Women were created to have the covering of a man. Men and women are on two different tracks or lanes, with both going in the same direction, and with the same divinely assigned destination. In many regards, they are alike, but simultaneously uniquely different. The differences are many, but the intent is that man and woman would undergird and complement each other while providing the physical and physiological support of the other.

When man stands flatfooted in his place and executes his dominion as ordained of God, displaying all the, "likeness," and attributes of God, following the relationship pattern God Himself modeled before him, then his relationship with the woman given to him will have the footing, foundation, and structure to sustain a healthy marriage. This is only one side. Women must resist being heady and high-minded, by walking in humility; accepting her Godly assignment no matter how unfair it appears. She must recognize her strengths are given to her to be a help meet to her husband; to undergird and motivate her man's ego so that his back will remain straight and his shoulders square as he positions himself under the God-assigned load he has been preordained to carry. She must become his soul's resting place, a sweet salve for all his woes, providing as a cool drink of water in the heat of the day, and as a dry towel ready to wipe the sweat from his brow. As his mate, void of a contentious spirit, she must toil with him, and by him, ensuring he becomes and remains sure-footed in the lane he has been given to have dominion over. Herein the woman is fulfilled, and the man is strengthened. Both are proud of and in their accomplishments, relationships, and their individual and collective lane assignments.

STRENGTH AND HONOR ARE HER CLOTHING; AND SHE SHALL REJOICE IN TIMES TO COME. SHE OPENS HER MOUTH WITH WISDOM; AND IN HER TONGUE IS THE LAW OF KINDNESS, SHE LOOKS WELL TO THE WAYS OF HER HOUSEHOLD AND DOES NOT EAT THE BREAD OF IDLENESS. HER CHILDREN ARISE UP, AND CALL HER BLESSED; HER HUSBAND ALSO AND HE PRAISES HER. (PROVERBS 31:25-28)

Pairing off a man and a woman simply due to their gender, with all its strict laws and punishments in the earlier years of mankind, had some success. Those successes were mainly because of the close circle of families and peers, coupled with a healthy respect for marriage and headship. However, many of these marriages had two faces, one at home and another outside. The struggle to maintain the integrity of marriage as dictated by the male, reasonable or unreasonable, often caused or gave men the liberty to become abusers to the wife and their children. Many married women found themselves held as sociological and physiological hostages. Without viable options, or the means of supporting themselves and their children, should they leave and end their marriage.

Many changes have taken place since those times, as new laws have been created to intervene on behalf of those living under such conditions. Yet the influences of these complicated marriages in the forties, fifties, and sixties, with the sweeping changes of the seventies and eighties, now reveal some strong unsettling rejections to marriage, manifested as fears of acceptance, and preposterous expectations of marriages today. The growing number of divorces heightens these fears, leaving many of today's youth rejecting the notion of marriage, opting rather to just live together.

Marriage is hard enough, even when two people love each other. Too often, they are left alone to work out their problems and hopefully get past their disagreements. The trouble that has brewed on the inside too often is unknown until it spills onto the outside. In our world today, there are too many options and side booths that exist simply to derail relationships, married or unmarried. The adversary is still roaming, seeking who or what he may devour. The mind is still Lucifer's preferred playground, where the lust of the eye and of the flesh offer endless possibilities, rather than man and woman choosing to work out their differences when pride shuts the doorway to communication.

Too often, our mates are selected using the wrong criteria. The first of which is their looks, the second their attributes, and the third their financial abilities or potential. Leaving them to only receive a beautiful face, a rugged body, and a financially secure nightmare. Too many of our men and women carry emotional scars from these relationships, and when the scars are unmasked, they leave hurt, bruised, and disillusioned partners in their wake.

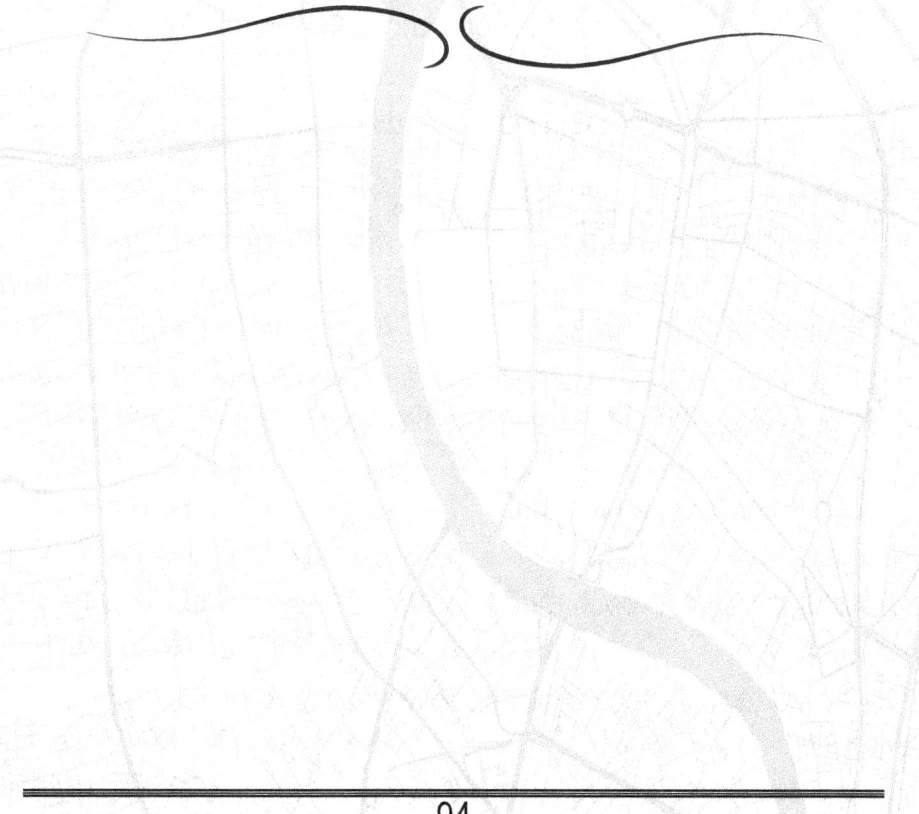

Hurt women will shut down and close-off. The pain from the detachment of a relationship is devastating, emotionally and physically. Relationships, no matter how deeply committed, or devoted, represent a personal investment; the loss of which most women will never fully recover.

Before she gets involved, there are some basic questions that she must ask herself:

What is it about him that appeals to me? Does he offer me a secure place for my emotions? Does he only appeal to the wild, crazy, unstable, and uninhibited side of me?

Can I live with him based on my emotions alone?

What are our relationship's pro's and con's?

Where could I end up if I follow him?

Why is he interested in me?

How does he look at me? Is it admiration?

Does he only think I am hot?

How does he approach me?

Is he polite and respectful around me and truly concerned about me?

Does he even think about or talk about where he is going or what is his dream for tomorrow or how he plans to achieve them?

Is he respectful of me, and what does he think about people?

What is his personality type?

Is he a brawler, a peacekeeper, a helper, etc.?

What type of people are his friends?

What type of music does he like?

Who does he talk to about what is important to him?

Does he ever go to Church?

What does he think about God?

Is he comfortable talking about God or the Bible?

What are the principles and foundations of his beliefs?

If I went out with him, where would he take me?

Does he have kids, does he contribute to their care, and does he spend time with them?

What does he say about the baby or babies' mommas?

Does he open and talk freely with me?

Does he listen to me when it is my turn to talk?

Does he welcome my input?

What preparations has he made for the future?

Where does he work?

What are his goals for the future?

Does he want me bad enough to wait for me, or is he a player?

Is he interested in me only because he notices how beautiful I am?

Does he want to use me solely to satisfy his lustful desires?

And finally, the important question, you must ask him:

If I were your wife, what would you expect of me, and as my husband, what can I expect of you?

His answer should not be flippant, nor should he have to fumble for the answer. Again, this is before he has your heart. Remember, this is your lane! The answer to these questions and many more will determine if you should allow yourself to become emotionally vulnerable with him before he gets your heart. Your inner soul and/or personal satisfaction, or dissatisfaction with the answers spoken or otherwise revealed will not only determine if he will be a suitable husband for you; but more importantly, should determine if you can be a suitable wife for him. It will clearly determine if this is the man you want to make decisions for you and your children.

As a society, we have lost the ability to reason and define purpose that comes with productive directions. We are deciding based on what we perceive or feel. These things are unstable, having no foundation or footing on which sound judgment can show us (manifest) truth, and truth manifests the fruits of sound judgment. To hook-up with someone on feelings and feelings alone will often leave one crying for fulfillment of all the other basic needs the two of you will need to have met. A marriage is more than two people reciting written or unwritten vows, moving in together, and the social, and legal liberty to make love. Soon you both will require more of the other than during your pre-marriage relationship. Honor and respect are key!

They are not only spoken, but also unspoken. They are lived, demonstrated, shown, and they say I am not simply with you, but my goal is to always uplift you. To the male, she will soon watch you to see more than the strength of your arms, and your desire for intimacy with her. She will begin searching for the strength of your love. How far will you go to please her? What will you do to protect her? Is she first in your life, or now that you have won her heart, does it appear you have moved on to the next challenge? Are you interested in building a nest with and for her, or are you too busy with work and other projects that she must wait until you find time for her?

How do you make her feel protected and secure? What sacrifices are you prepared to make to better provide for a family? Can you both agree on what is important in your marriage?

As a wife, you are expected to blend with him, walk where he walks, and go where he goes. His conduct needs to be pleasing to you and soothing to your spirit. You are expected to become his helpmate as he becomes your covering. Knowing where he is going will allow you to aid him in what he will need to become successful during your journey together. Believe me, he will soon require more of you than to look pretty and meet his physical needs. You will build your world and family with him, and give yourself to him, as each of your needs are fulfilled. And finally, you will take his name and forsake your family name. As you are no longer a single woman connected to your father as your covering, but just as God brought Eve to Adam and presented her to him, hopefully your father or father-figure will present you to your husband as your covering. You are to find security in his love, and with him, that even when he is not with you, you will feel and bask in his love. No longer will you feel the physical vulnerability that has accompanied you when you were alone, but there is a newfound security at the base of your being, because you know he will come for you if you are afraid. He will do everything in his ability to rescue you if you are lost.

Yes, it sounds like a beautiful story, almost like a fairy tale. But for it to come true, there must be a decision within the woman and the man to accept, reverence and respect the biblical role of a woman. First, understanding she was created to meet a man's needs when given to the man (Genesis 2:20-25). Second, a woman's desire shall be to her husband. Third, her husband has authority over the wife (Genesis 3:16). Fourth, wives must submit to her husband, for the husband is the head of the wife, and she is charged with respecting her husband (Ephesians 5:22-33). This is not a one-sided or one-dimensional relationship. There is an equally biblical response and legislated requirement of the husband. But first, let's explore not what it sounds like, but what it means:

Woman was created as the helpmate for the husband. HE REALLY NEEDS YOU!! After Adam named all the animals, the birds, and the trees, the light of his continuance within him was going out. God recognized it and knew he needed something else, something more than work. For God, this something was the creation and relationship of the indwelling spirit being Adam. Adam being flesh, needed the accompaniment of another human form, capable of radiating and depositing light-like life into his being. Nothing does for a man what a loving woman does to his character, his manhood, self-esteem, and ultimately, his ego. Without a woman, man's inner light reflects loneliness, barrenness, lacks genuine passion, and purpose. The most universally-accepted and agreed upon statement of man across the continent is that: "as difficult as it is for a man to live with a woman, men cannot live without them."

After God had all the animals passed in review before Adam, none were a suitable helpmate. God created for Adam, "a woman," and fashioned her for him. God did not simply make the woman, but fashioned her solely for man. Nothing exceeds the woman's outer beauty more than her inner beauty, qualities, and charm. God endowed the woman with that special something that can melt a man's inner core and bring him to his knees, or send him with a smile, causing him to rush through his day to get home to her. The woman has caused many wars, and has been the reason many men have lost everything, including their lives, in defense or pursuit of her.

This type of power and ultra-positioning of the women in God's creation must be controlled with moral boundaries that will restrict the mind and flesh to a lane clearly defined, and yet, allow for the fulfillment and appreciation of her unique abilities, qualities, and gifting. First, God presented her to her husband, Adam, naked and unashamed, as a gift. What she is and what she has been given, which includes her gifts, are for her husband. This was further explained after the fall of man, where Lucifer used Eve to derail God's plan for human posterity. Second, a woman is not a free agent to do as she reasons, thinks, and/or pleases. She is expected to move and act within the boundaries (lane restrictions) of the husband as to his plans, heart, wishes, and desires. The woman's desires shall be to help her husband achieve his desires. Third, all that you desire shall be fulfilled in and through your husband. This then, would imply that out of your husband's love and respect for you, he will seek to dwell with you, his wife, according to his knowledge of you. (1 Peter 3:7; Ephesians 5:22-33).

His rule over you does not make you his slave, or he your master. But it is impossible for two people to live together out of the assumption of being equal, as both have an equal say in all matters. Mankind was not created with gender equality. Let us again examine the evidence. As Adam came first, given dominion, and Eve being taken from Adam and brought to Adam and given to Adam, and Adam having to answer to God for the conduct of himself and Eve, and finally, the ultimate assignment to women that her husband shall be in charge. Genesis 3:16 says, "thy desire shall be to thy husband," and Colossians 3:18 says, "women submit yourselves unto thy own husband." These scriptures negate the Idea of gender equality.

Man must be recognized in his rightful place as the head or having the ultimate decision-making authority. It is his lane. With that said, however, it is necessary for two people to discuss, give opinions, and their reasons to the why they favor one direction over the other.

The wife, as the, "help mate," and partner, must be given the opportunity to express and fully communicate her views and thoughts. However, peace and harmony in being overruled can only be maintained if the wife has already made up her mind that she will submit and surrender to the biblical position and assigned headship of her husband. This is not a decision to make with each major or minor crisis, but a decision that must be made during the courtship. The woman must ask herself and be sure of her answer: "Is this someone I am comfortable with making decisions for me, and will I be willing to accept his direction for my life and our children?"

However, something that seemed to work in twenty-century families was assignments of responsibility. According to each partner's experiences, training, or absolute concerns, they are assigned that area of responsibility for the family. These arrangements seem to make the best use of each partner's abilities and allow each member an opportunity to be fulfilled in the areas of their greatest concern and expertise. This seems to work and provides an alternative solution if neither partner acts without the others' knowledge. It also appears to answer the question: does the father know best?

Yes, man came first, and God intentionally formed him in His image and likeness. Man is to reflect the image and likeness of God, and to know and exhibit the attributes of God. Man is to mimic the ways of God on Earth, to direct and lead mankind to godly knowledge, worship, and order. God Himself is so invested in this exalted position of man that throughout the Old Testament, the males were required, both men and boys, to step away from worldly involvement, to come at an appointed time, to turn aside solely unto Him for reflection and mentoring. A refresher course in, "Godliness 101," staged and directed by God Himself. Man made in the image of God, is collectively representative as little gods, reflecting God on the earth.

In the image of God, man is creative, engineering, administrative, dominating, and subduing. He is lord over and ruler over all that God has revealed to him. In the likeness of God, he is to be loving, kind, gentle, compassionate, discerning, having authority, possessing judgment, exhibiting grace, demonstrating mercy, and being long-suffering.

This is the model, as a gentle giant, that God presents the woman too. These are the attributes that she should find in a man she will call her husband. He should first recognize her as a marvel, wonderfully made for him; then praise, and give honor to God for bringing her to him. Man's level of respect for her should first start with gratitude toward God.

As Lucifer allowed his beauty, godly positioning, talents, and gifts to inwardly corrupt him, Lucifer then turned his attention from God onto himself. Wherein, he sought the opportunity to elevate himself and place his throne above the throne of God. This inner perversion brought on a rebellion against God, for which he was rightly rejected from heaven. Too many of our men and women find themselves as human beings blindly following the same path to self-destruction. Each generation, building on the declinations of the past, finds new ways and depths of defiance to the ways and order of our Creator. So much so, have we turned to blind ambitions that our leaders are truly toiling over, "What came first, the chicken, or the egg?"

As we move further and further away from the truth, the knowledge of God, our Creator, and the lanes for which we were designed for His purpose, we elevate ourselves to self-glory and praise, seeking for ways to disqualify Him.

In pursuit of life's ambitions and goals, many men will descend to any level or means possible to achieve their individual desires, financial standings, or status. Natural man finds little or no need for God. Because man has distanced himself from God, man finds God too distant for man to reason, comprehend, relate to, or put his trust in. But God yet offered to man an appeal, "Return unto Me, and I will return to you."

Too many of us think that God is unnatural; He is not tangible. We cannot see Him with the naked eye, nor handle Him with our hands. We can't put Him against our lips, or in our mouths to taste Him. Nor can we put Him under a magnifying glass or test tube to find Him. However, because the knowledge of Him has not been passed on as the true and living God; of whom we must come to know and accept in the spirit, it is impossible to know Him. For His Word says He is a spirit, and we must come to know Him in spirit and in truth.

The spirit is not only that in which He breathes into us as the breath of life and causes us to become living souls, but also that which makes us most like Him, and identifies us with Him. For we too are spirit beings, composed of mind, body, and soul. Our spirit is the God/Man connection, and the place of connection that is satisfied, at peace, and fulfilled when we are in the right connection and standing with God. The spirit of man is within the body; an existing invisible organ where the invisible God is made manifest and glorified on earth. It is the place where the Holy Spirit takes up residency and seals us until that great day of God's redemptive plan is complete. Man without God is an empty and dangerous creature, a danger to himself, and mankind. He is operating without control, guidance, leadership, or accountability. To him, there is no proper lane, only what he deems profitable or advantageous to himself. As humans seek their own roads, remember, "There is a way that seems right to a man; but the end thereof leads to destruction."

Far too many of our men have fallen under the influence of Lucifer, having gotten drunk on, "little god," authority, and dominion. They now chart their own course, using and abusing this dominion and authority for their own good pleasure to satisfy their lust and greed, becoming heady, high-minded, truce breakers, lovers of themselves rather than of God, out of control, void of self-discipline, and self-respect. (2 Timothy 2:2-4)

Men are first attracted to the physical, fleshly form of the female, and it is for this reason women seeking a mate spend a great deal of time making themselves as attractive as possible. It is truly the gift of God, for God has ordained it to be so. Unmistakably so, a woman was made for man, and he is to be attracted to her and only to her. But a man who gets lost in the physical beauty of a woman will often miss the genuine gift; that is a soft, sweet, gentle, loving, caring, pleasing, charming, smiling spirit that will claim residency in his heart and memory. As it lingers, it will permeate his being and soften his natural heart. The right woman completes the soul of a man. Her mental and physical essence is like the hand of God at work reinserting the perfectly formed rib he took from Adam, not on his side, but at his side. The right woman makes a man's heart joyous. The reflection of his happiness completes the woman who has found the love of a man she desires and opens to him the treasures of her love.

Understanding this, it is wise to caution men to operate in the natural model of which God created and intended. However, as in the beginning, when the fallen angels beheld the beauty of women, lusted for them, and took them to satisfy their lust, many women at the hands of men seeking only self-gratification, with tongues of angels, and the smooth subtlety of Lucifer (Satan)... have tainted the gentle fruit of many women, leaving only a beautiful shell of which some women commonly refer to as, "This," (her body). Like fruit that sours on the vine, many women have been abused and misused during their childhood by unscrupulous men, and yes, even at the hands of other family members. The emotional pain and/or attempts to cover such invisible pain have left psychological, physiological, and invisible disfiguring scar tissue, thus consuming the root and stem of what was her genuine beauty. Many of these women are angry at themselves and have a closed heart. They feel only distrust and disdain for men. The anger consumes them, leaving a cold-hearted shell in its place.

For most men, there is the ability to bounce back from the hurt and pain of a broken relationship, to collect their pride, remember the memories, learn from their mistakes, and prepare for the next relationship. However, it is not the same for women. She is created from the emotion God has for man and is an emotional being. Her first thought is to regret being open and vulnerable to the possibility of hurt. This openness and vulnerability are precisely what must happen for the woman to get involved in a relationship. With little forethought, the woman is tempted, after being hurt and/or humiliated, to find a way to hurt him back. If there is no closure and healing, she will close, and hide herself from potential emotional meltdowns. To move on, she must allow herself to become vulnerable again. Why? Because along with her emotions come attachments and an avalanche of dreams, aspirations, expectations, and possibilities, all of which defy what she sees happening around her, with her friends and in her family. She must deal with an onslaught of questions that all come rushing at her simultaneously. Could this be the one, despite his charm and appeal, does he have other motives, and/or is he seriously looking for a monogamous relationship or just another challenge? Women must be smarter and willing to go beyond what looks good, attractive, and other forms of personal appeal when pursued by a male who might sweep her off her feet. How did he perfect his irresistible charm and charisma? Become an investigator; proceed with caution. That is your lane.

Pairing off a man and a woman simply because of their gender, with all its strict laws and punishments in the earlier days, had some success. Those successes were mainly due to the close circle of families and peers, coupled with a healthy respect for marriage and headship. However, many of these marriages had two faces, one at home and the one the world views.

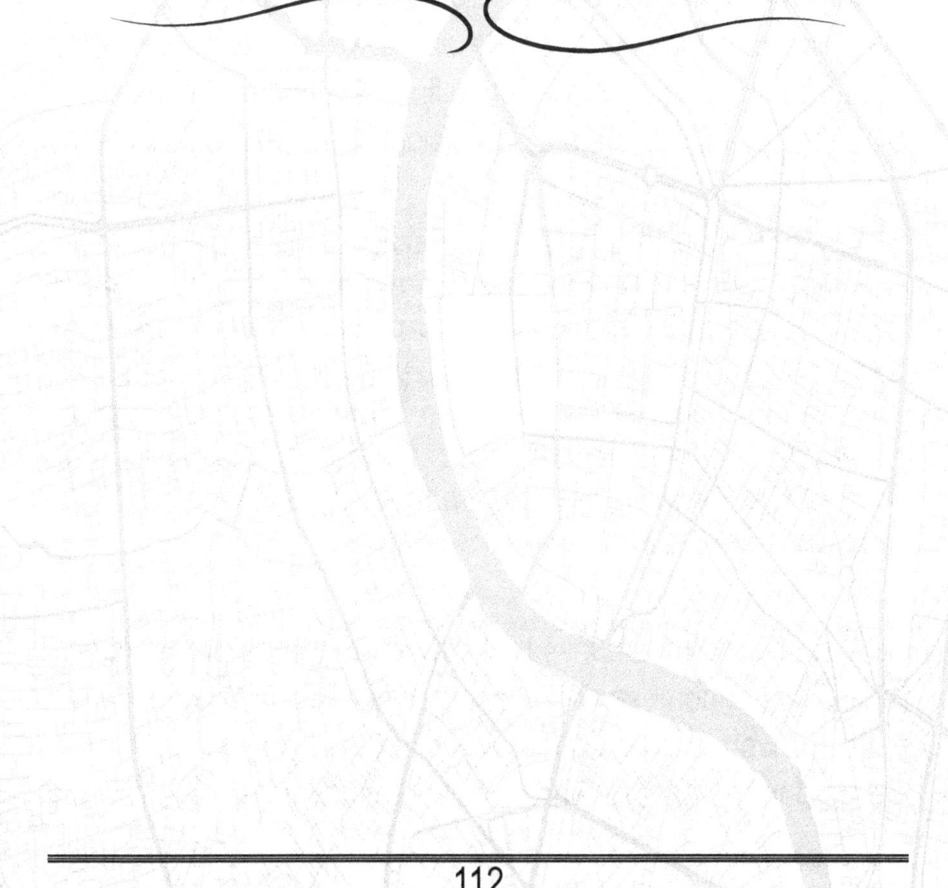

It is a natural thing for a man to desire a woman, and for a woman to desire and submit to physical intimacy with a man. For this cause, the woman was created and intended to be the mother of humanity. For it is by this means, the attraction of man to woman, that God has ordained the perpetual replenishing and reproducing of humanity. Scientific research into the human body has revealed each of us has a natural propensity toward sexual intimacy. This is the libido, and it affects and summons us biologically, psychologically, and physiologically. This propensity toward human mating is further reinforced in creating the man with testosterone, and the female with estrogen. Which is further evidence that we as humans are sexual beings. However, the attraction of a male to a female and a female to a male is not a green light stuck on go, but is first the innate compass that prompts humanity to be mated with only humankind.

And Adam gave names to all cattle, and to the fowl of the air, and to every beast of the field; but for Adam there was not found a help meet for him. And the Lord God caused a deep sleep to fall upon Adam, and he slept: and he took one of his ribs, and closed the flesh instead thereof; And the rib, which the Lord God had taken from man, made he a woman, and brought her unto the man. (Genesis 2:20-22)

So, it is this truth compass that directs man away from animals (bestiality), or homosexuality, and points him to a just and proper mate of a woman. The woman was made and fashioned solely for man. Adam, in the pre-plan of God, was fashioned and created to mate with the later-created creature, woman (no further operation was needed). This distinctive lane compass also says God made only one woman for Adam and brought her alone to him to fulfill all his needs. Further, we need to understand both are committed to each other. Before Adam knew her as his wife and dedicated himself to her as his charge, spoken or unspoken, there was a covenant relationship. God created her for him, brought her to him, gave her to him, and ordained her as his wife. Hence, we find further instructions in (Genesis 2:24), "Therefore, a man should leave his mother and father and cleave to his wife." That one man with one woman in the covenant relationship of marriage should come together to reproduce. (Genesis 1:28) says, "...and God blessed them and said unto them be fruitful, multiply and replenish the earth".

There was never a mention of Adam going to surgery to be equipped with male reproduction organs and abilities. Therefore, to accommodate the man, she was created with him in mind. There has never been a reason for an alternative or substitute for what God has ordained. Any other means of intimacy, male to male or female to female, even now being sanctioned and legitimized by man, is an abomination to our Creator. (A slap in the face, and total disrespect of His creative plan for humankind, and outside the prescribed lane.)

According to our scriptures, the act of sexual intercourse is first and foremost for the reproduction of humankind and animal-kind with their own kind according to God's creative plan. However, the enticement to mate is the physiological and physical promise of pleasure. Henceforth, the reproduction process is both pleasurable and gratifying. We can consider this a bonus or a sexual side-effect. Not only is the attraction preordained, but also the reproduction process of which a man carries within him the seed that must be deposited within the female, where in the egg awaits the fertilization of the male seed. This then is known as penetration or sexual intercourse. In this process, the female willingly (not by force) admits or allows the male to penetrate her with his male instrument or penis, at the female opening or the vagina. Whether knowingly or unknowingly, fertilization occurs when God determines after the male seed is deposited within the female, and the process of impregnation begins its work.

Once it begins, the process will not pause to ask the questions, whether you are in a relationship, whether you love each other, whether you or your mating partner from this relationship are ready to become or expect to become parents or not. The biological result of sex has far more lasting consequences than the promise of pleasure, or the bliss of personal gratification. Like animals, our animalistic nature will always prompt us to consummate the act of mating. Problem is, as we are similar to animals, prone to animalistic behaviors, we are not animals. As humans, we should each hold ourselves to a higher standard, discipline, and conduct as humans, having a sense of self-control, and reasoning beyond our raw feelings and desires.

For every action, there is a reaction with consequences we may not be ready for or be mature enough and prepared to handle.

So, we can conclude from this that sexual intercourse, and the primary purpose for sex, was and still is to reproduce (i.e., bring forth children and replenish the earth) (Genesis 1:28). The issue is the recognition that at times man is stuck on go and considers it a bonus.

The bonus is that sexual intimacy brings with it a strong possibility of impregnation, entreats us while mating with great physical pleasure, and enjoyment, climaxing with extreme gratification and fulfillment for both the male and female. Researchers tell us that there are thousands of pleasure nerve endings within the male and female body dedicated to the achievement of sexual pleasure and stress relief from intercourse. It is for this cause, along with its innate enticements, as mentioned above, that we as humans have majored in the minors: the bonus, and reduced to the minor, that which was and should always be major; or at least considered in the equation; the possibility of impregnation. From that union, a child is expected to be conceived through parenthood. These two are in your lane:

Know ye that in the last days perilous times shall come, for men shall be lovers of their own selves, without natural affection, lovers of pleasure more than lovers of God. (2 Timothy 3:2,4)

In times past, the joy of the news of one having conceived and the excitement of a woman's ability to bear a child echoed throughout the neighborhood. Many husbands were patted on the back and elevated to sit in the circle of men in his community. As custom dictated, the women of her family assisted with the furnishings in the expected couple's home, those things that the baby might need. They await the birth of the baby with great anticipation. The father, having taken serious responsibility for the birth of his seed, as the provider, promotes himself to a better position to provide for the mother of his child and the child.

Sex today between both married couples and the single, is no longer considered the means of procreating. Society has demeaned the act to be one of pleasure and release and not for the purposes of conception. Fewer participants anticipate parenthood; that a child representing that union might be born into the world and shared by the two in a loving relationship. If we examine the overwhelming statistics today, we find pregnancy is often considered a disappointment, tragedy, unexpected burden, an unjust and undue consequence of which neither participant wanted nor expected. Rather, it was all about pleasure, simply a physical act between two or more people that brought pleasure and gratification while playing roulette with the chances of pregnancy.

Consequences of these chances show up in considerable numbers, just to mention a few: sexually transmitted diseases, unwanted pregnancies that ended in over 998,000 legal abortions in the United States in 2014; fathers denying paternity and shirking their responsibility never committing to fatherhood, resulting in paternity testing, and court-ordered child support; single-parent homes run by women as head-of-household, with malnourished children; families living at or below the poverty line who often experience intervention by Child Welfare and/or Child Social Services; many child abuse and neglect cases, cases of child adoption and placement; a lust and passion-driven society; out-of-control teens and adults who become unprepared and ill-equipped parents; families with multiple fathers and/or mothers; runaway and/or homeless children; and explosive relationships built on passion; and families dependent upon state-sponsored childcare.

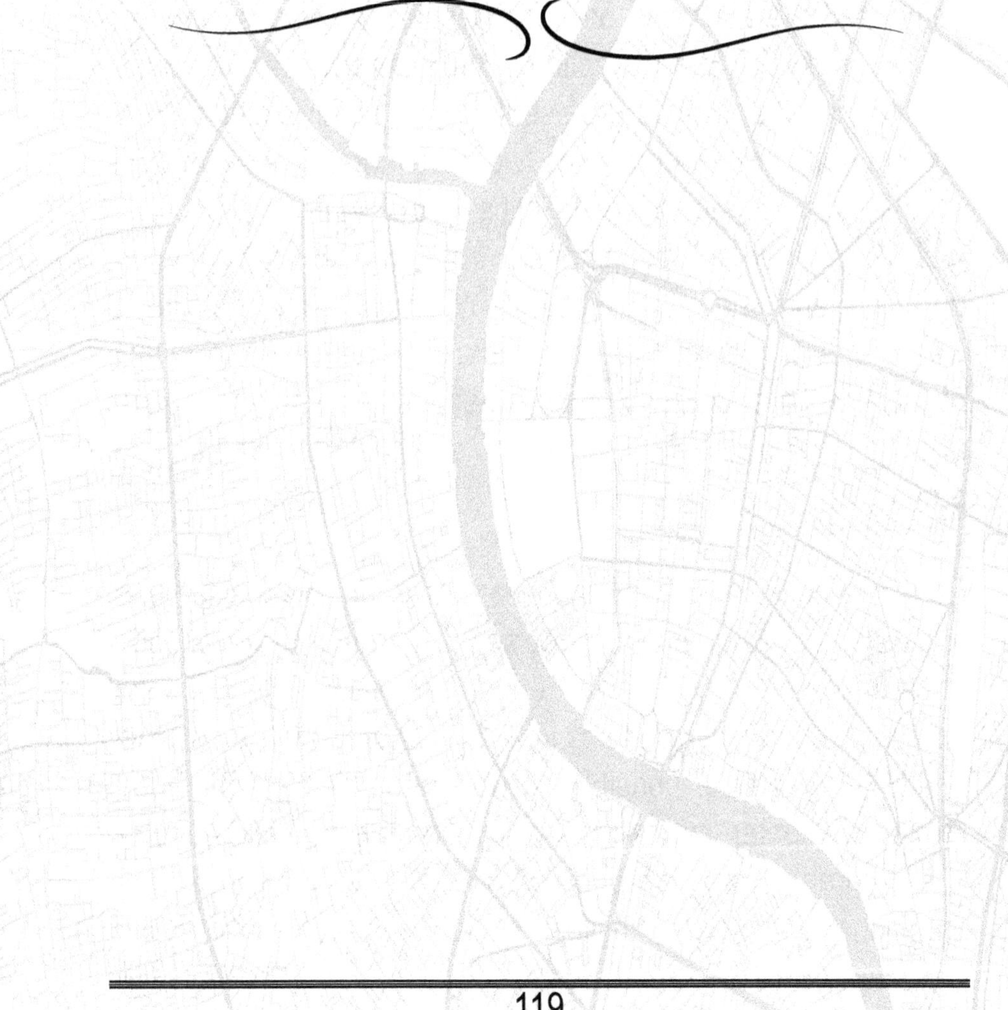

Each of us has the gift to procreate, and the ability to give and receive tremendous pleasure in the intimacy of a fleshly union. It is no accident, our Creator has equipped mankind to perpetuate the next generation. Surely, we will be responsible with our gifts; not only our abilities; but also with every precious seed we have been given to sow, and that awaits fertilization in a far-reaching and protected region of the female body; and it is not to be taken lightly! Every seed, whether sown in love or a casual experience, bears each man's DNA, must be recognized, and accepted by its gifted carrier! As the man, he is not only the carrier of the reproduction seeds, but also the lifelong protector, provider, and overseer of that seed that carries his image. Whether it reaches its mark, whether it is wasted, or produces a child, it is his seed, issued, numbered, and stamped to him. He is accountable and responsible for his seed, and where it lands in the woman. As it represents his strength, he, now in its infant state, must become his strength. As it grows, it becomes his responsibility to shape it and function as its provider, which encompasses the provision and protection of the woman that carries his seed to term. This is HIS lane!

The woman's assignment is the same. She has a number of eggs nestled within her inner body. Her decision to open her body removes the outer guard, leaving not only her, but her eggs vulnerable, and approachable by the seed of man. Her decision to open herself carries with it not only her acknowledgement of her want and need, but also her consent to the possibility of pregnancy. Knowing that the seed would have no other route to her precious eggs than her, allowing the male to penetrate her. The man, whether he loves her or not, once sexually gratified, can leave with or without a loving attachment; and too often, when he does, it is very possible that he may carry with him no physical or psychological consequence of the consummation. But the woman's eggs are precious, not simply because they are the eggs assigned to her; but the sperm he leaves behind upon ejaculation (climax) once mating with her egg is pre- genetically designed to lead to a pregnancy. This means that there is a high possibility that a child will spend nine months growing inside of her. The consequences of pregnancy are sure; everything in your life will be called to change, whether you are ready for his or her birth. This child conceived in a moment of pleasure, will spend the rest of their childhood as your responsibility, as will your life as a mother responsible for the wellbeing of that child, will change.

It is a woman's godly assignment that together with a loving, responsible mate, preferably a husband, that she will eventually become a mother. Until then, the woman has a responsibility to herself and the potential child to choose the right conditions under which motherhood should accrue. She must always be disciplined, guarded, and protective not only of her present days, but of her future as well. This is not only the proper order, but also HER lane!

Many will only wink at these words of wisdom and advice, but wisdom says to you, do not contribute to the growing problem of unwanted children and the staggering number of abortions. The market is now flooded with devices that protect from sexually transmitted diseases and prevent unwanted pregnancies. If you must be sexually active outside of marriage, be responsible and prepared before sex to be accountable for your SEED.

Women, as your bodies house the reproductive organs where impregnation begins and facilitate the growth and development of what will become a fetus and soon a child ready to be born, you must protect yourself and your EGGS from unwanted impregnation. This too is your lane.

It is a man-made expression of political correctness designed to give a name and category to a human choice in mating that previously had no acceptable title. It fills the verbal void between that which is understood as acceptable and the unacceptable. While it provides a shelter under which one's civil rights are protected. It is called an abomination to man's creator God. (Leviticus 18:22, 20:13)

As God created the woman and brought her to man, it is clear the intended relationship is to be the pairing of a man to a woman, male to female. Further, they were told to be fruitful and multiply. The laying together of a man to man or woman to woman negates and denies the natural purpose and process of which mating and the attraction to mate were intended. The natural penetrating organ of the male is not for another male; it is unnatural, unproductive, and a perversion of that part of the body, which was designed not to be penetrated; but to enable the body to discharge waste. The same is the case with the female. She was created to be penetrated by the male, so that the seed of the male could find and mate with the egg hidden within the female body and accessible at the designed opening.

In this day and time in which we live, the thoughts and ways of man now dictate what is right or wrong. Man seems to be saying to our creator God, "We can take it from here! We disagree with what You and the church have instructed us to do, and Your desires will no longer dictate to us what is right, wrong, just, or unjust. We are no longer concerned with what is pleasing to God our Creator, nor with what is right in His eyes. We have become of age and without concern for what pleases You; but rather what seems right and acceptable to this broad society where everyone should be included, and acceptable regardless of their gender, agender, practice or lifestyle.

It is a very noble gesture to fight for the liberty and inclusiveness of all people. But we must know and consider the reason that society has closed its ranks on certain influences that are against the natural as explained above (Paragraph II) and brings with it the consequences that societies embrace. In this case the biblical expression, “A little leaven will leaven the whole lump,” (Mathew 13:33) truly applies. Meaning; thoughts, ideals, principles, or practices that are injected into our society have the ability over time to change or alter it completely. Exchanging the truth for a lie and the natural for the unnatural. Not always spoken by those who are given over to this lifestyle, but many will confess that they may be partnered with someone of their lifestyle. They are truly seeking, “a straight person.” In other words, “your sons and daughters.”

This generation is already being desensitized by laws that allow the raising of children in same-sex homes, and our TV and Movie industry now are showing explicit scenes of intimate same-sex relationships in the very act. What our society has rejected as unnatural is now being modeled to our children as natural, and bringing with it the judgment and penalties the likes of that which fell on Sodom and Gomorrah.

"Now the men of Sodom were very wicked and were sinning against the Lord exceedingly." (Genesis 13:13,18:20)

And before they had gone to bed, "All the men from every part of the city of Sodom, young and old, surrounded the house. They called to Lot, "where are the men that came to you tonight, bring them out to us, so that we can have sex with them". And Lot went out to meet them, and closed the door behind him and said "(NO) my friends, do not do this wicked thing." Then the two men said to Lot, "Get all of your kinspeople out of here because we are about to destroy this place. The outcry of the Lord against this people is so great that he has sent us to destroy it." By the time Lot reached Zoar, the sun was up then the Lord rained down burning sulfur upon the land. He overthrew all those cities, and all the plain, and all of the inhabitants, and vegetation in the land." (Genesis 19:4-13,23-25)

In the book of Romans, we find this record.

"They neither glorified Him as God nor gave thanks to Him, but their thinking became futile and their foolish hearts became darkened. Although they claimed to be wise, they became fools and exchanged the glory of the immortal God for images made to look like mortal man. Therefore, God gave them over to their sinful desires of their hearts to sexual impurity for the degrading of their bodies with one another. They exchanged the truth of God for a lie and worshiped and served created things... Because of this God gave them over to shameful lust

THE SINFUL DESIRES OF THEIR HEART TO SEXUAL PERVERSION. EVEN THEIR WOMEN EXCHANGED NATURAL RELATIONSHIPS FOR UNNATURAL ONES, IN THE SAME WAY THE MEN ABANDONED NATURAL RELATIONSHIPS WITH WOMEN AND WERE INFLAMED WITH LUST FOR ONE ANOTHER, MEN COMMITTING INDECENT ACTS WITH OTHER MEN AND RECEIVING WITHIN THEMSELVES DUE PENALTIES FOR THEIR PERVERSION. THEREFORE, SINCE THEY DID NOT THINK IT WORTHWHILE TO RETAIN THE KNOWLEDGE OF GOD, HE GAVE THEM OVER TO DEPRAVED MINDS TO DO WHAT OUGHT NOT TO BE DONE. THEY WERE FILLED WITH ALL KINDS OF WICKEDNESS, GREED AND DEPRAVITY. THEY WERE FILLED WITH EVERY KIND OF EVIL, MURDER, AND STRIFE, DECEIT, AND MALICE. THEY BECAME GOSSIPERS, SLANDERERS, GOD HATERS, INSOLENT, ARROGANT AND BOASTFUL. THEY INVENTED NEW WAYS OF DOING EVIL, THEY WERE DISOBEDIENT TO THEIR PARENTS, SENSELESS, FAITHLESS, HEARTLESS, AND RUTHLESS. ALTHOUGH THEY KNEW GOD'S RIGHTEOUS DECREE, THEY KNEW THAT THOSE WHO WOULD DO SUCH A THING DESERVE DEATH, THEY NOT ONLY CONTINUED TO DO THESE VERY THINGS BUT ALSO APPROVED OF THOSE WHO PRACTICED THEM." (ROMANS 1:21-32)

A word of caution: We are not the first generation that in spite of our knowledge of God; no longer desire to be influenced by what is in His book. The word, "abomination," of which there is a great deal of debate in and outside the church today, appears many times in scripture, and commonly relates to the acts or practices of man referred to as ungodly, i.e., adultery, lying, stealing, mistreating a neighbor, or abusing authority. However, sexual sins denote a requirement of a completely different connotation, "because they pervert," the designed order of God's creation and His laws of nature in favor of that which in His sight is unnatural.

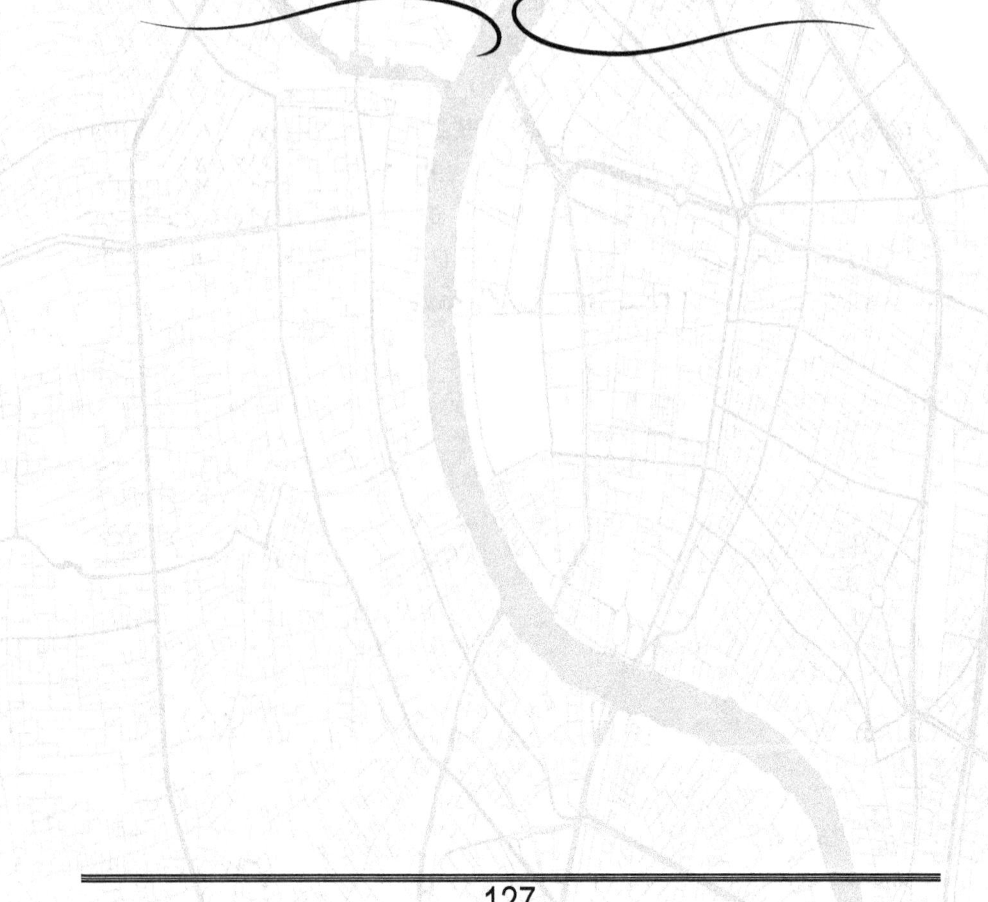

A baby is born; to some, there are mixed emotions; to others there is immense joy at this miracle of life. But have you ever considered that to the baby there is considerable trauma and shock upon delivery? All that they have ever known throughout their fetal existence, no matter how good, bad, or uncomfortable, has now been snatched from around them. Their comfort zone is gone. Everything is brand new and frightening. Their nervous system goes into overload as the brain struggles to make sense of all that has happened. The brain not yet capable of comprehending, and finding no data to explain, sounds an alarm that now shakes the entire infant body. This high-pitched and shrill alarm heightens the shock and fear that now completely consumes this newly transitioned creature. The fear, along with the void of answers, now sends the body into an enormous level of stress, which is manifested as trapped energy frantically seeking a means of release. Unknown to the child, there is a pre-programmed psycho-physical response system that for the next 6-8 months will be this newly born child's only means of outwardly expressing the traumatic fear or unanswered needs within the child; the baby begins to cry!!!

Do you know that this baby, who eventually grows into a small child and too soon a pre-teen, never stops crying? Even into the years as a teenager and young adult, they are still crying. Fact is, if the questions first posed at birth are not satisfactorily answered and put to rest, many full-grown adults will become psychologically crippled mentally, and emotionally, developmentally dwarfed, with low self-esteem, and socially-handicapped.

Let's examine the questions of which the answers properly demonstrated will bring a sense of peace and tranquility to a newborn. Let us consider that the answers, when properly modeled, applied, and/or reinforced throughout childhood, can settle the eruption of unsettled energies bubbling like a physiological volcano within your child's nervous systems, especially of those still in the tender years.

Here, crying relates not to the outer flow of tears; but to the endless almost hysterical heart and soul need for inner peace; a need for a settlement with questions regarding their security, and an assurance that allows him/her to feel loved, accepted, and included with real value in the society of humans. These questions may be presented differently at each stage of growth and development, but stem from the same or similar list of needs.

Your child's repeated questions, as a parent, your answers need to reflect on what happened.

What happened?

You could no longer grow in your mother's tummy.

Am I safe here?

It's OK, for you to be here.

Is this alright?

Mommy and daddy will make it alright.

Will I be alright?

You can relax, we will take care of you.

Will I be alone?

No, you belong to us, and we belong to you.

Is this strange place friendly?

This strange place will be your home. You are safe!

Will I be accepted here?

You are accepted. We want you.

Am I going to be loved?

Yes, so very much. We will prove it to you.

Am I going to be taken care of?

Yes, we will let nothing bad happen to you.

Can I have my warm cover again?

You have a new warm and fuzzy cover called home.

Who are these strange creatures?

We are your family. We will surround you and care for you.

Will they take care of me?

Yes, we are here with you, and for you, always.

Can I find anything familiar here?

Yes, you will always be part of Mommy and Daddy.

How do I make this adjustment?

We will help you every step of the way.

Why is the child crying?

The simple term is affirmation: never has one single word carried so much weight, nor been so inclusive of our children's greatest need.

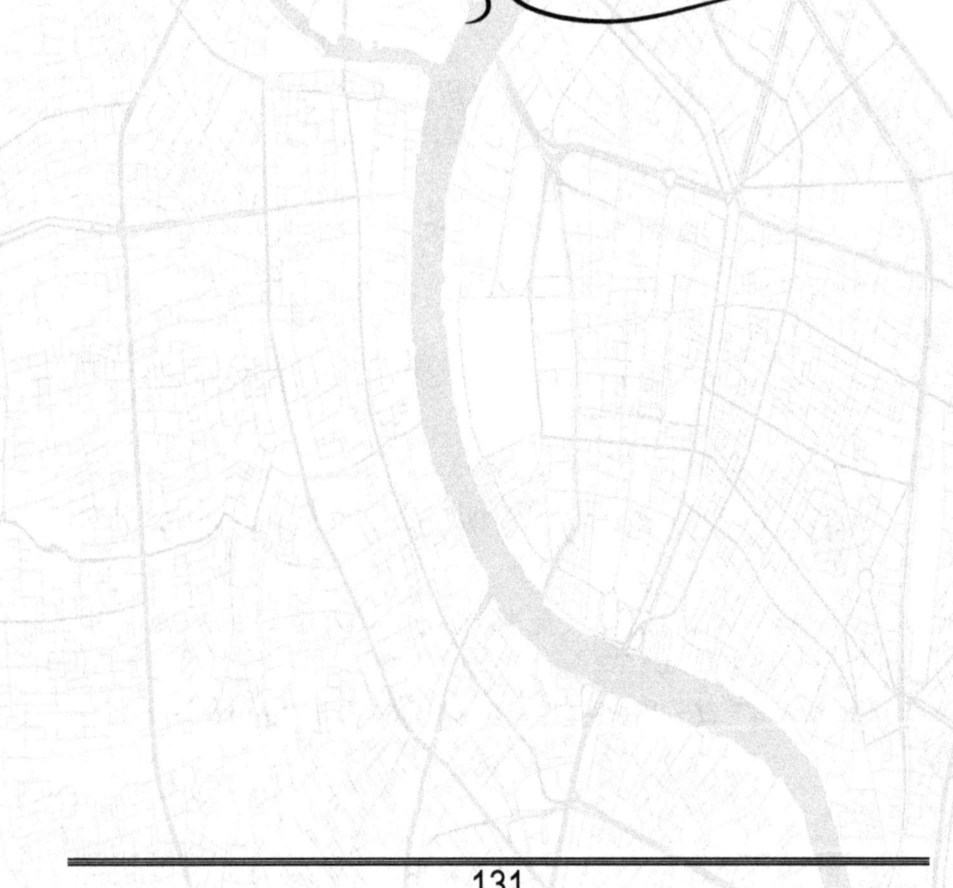

All the moving, breathing, working, and even resting elements of our world depend on energy. We would like to think of the energy boom of the Industrial era, where many of today's energy sources were tapped, harvested, and industrialized; but the truth is, energy has been around since what we know as the beginning of time. In Genesis Chapter 1:2, we find that at the depth of our energy search, which is the beginning, a Spirit (energy) moved on the face of the waters. That Spirit Being, God, was not only the source of energy, but also the conductor from which all things were formed, made, created, and energized.

His creative ability to change what was, and to bring into existence what was not, by the power of His spoken Word, reveals to us a Spirit Being of energy; a Force that moved and arranged both the then present and the created energies to His own good pleasure. "And God said!" (Genesis 1:3). Many refute the belief that even today, His spoken and written Word still has energy. If we further examine the creative energy of God, we find all He created from His energy has energy.

The Sun has energy not only to maintain an orbit, but it is also an internal source of energy. It gives light and warms the universe as we know it. The waters have energy, from which the waters are a divided firmament in the heavens, while maintaining the set boundaries in the seas from overflowing the earth. The Earth has energy from which it maintains a gravitational pull, producing gems, fine stones, fuels, and minerals of all kinds. These are just a few of the obvious places' mankind finds energy. But, in all truth, energy is found in all places where we can trace God. In

His word and His deeds, there is evidence of energy. (Genesis 1:2-27)

And God breathed into man the, "living, energized breath of life," and man became a living soul! (Genesis 2:7). Man, as a created being, is energy, has energy, and has a body, soul, and spirit, which in turn is subject to energies. Energy is active, pushing, pulling, guiding, controlling, restricting, releasing, restraining, exploding, rejecting, affirming, and reproving. Yet energy consistently requires discipline and balance and has its own disciplines. Energy can be positive or negative, good, or bad, and/or constructive or destructive.

Nowhere in our universe is this presence of energy more evident than in human beings (God's created beings). Yet, nowhere else in this vast universe is this truth more ignored than in us as human beings! Most particularly in the need for conscientious, on purpose, parenting (the directing, balancing, and challenging of our children's energies).

Our failure to recognize and understand the presence of energies, especially the traumatic energies from negative experiences, or repeated traumas, too often in our homes and families, left unattended, unbalanced, and unchallenged, distort the intended images of what was to be in our children. Many of today's homes are full of negative energies, confusion, unsettled, unloving, without natural affection, strife, hatred, racial tension, unemployment, hunger, substance abuse, and substandard conditions, just to name a few. The energies from these negative experiences, left trapped in your child's psyche and nervous system, leave strong and lasting effects on a child's emotions. The shadows of which become etched on the ever-learning canvas of a child's mind, and ultimately their nervous system. These displaced, negative energies eventually become radically visible in our children's behavior; evidence of parental neglect and/or mismanagement in an unsettled child's conduct.

These negative energies desperately need to be balanced with positive energies, sometimes as simple as a hug, a smile, or a reassurance of order and stability with the intervention of others more settled, or a temporary retreat to a place of order, compassion, or quinine concern. Nothing is more damaging to a child than repeated fighting between mother and father, significant others, or siblings. Yet the parent who uses profanity (a form of spoken negative energy) when addressing a child or looks at a child with disdainment (transference of mental energy) ranks alongside these immense nerve and confidence destroyers. These imbalances, left unchanged, oftentimes leave the child ill-equipped to meet the waiting society of their tomorrow as wholesome, physically, psychologically, and emotionally equipped, men and women capable of facing the challenges and difficulties of an unforgiving, unequal, and ever-changing world.

Energies, as modeled by each parent, and are transferable to their child. Energy must be challenged and handled with significant consideration. One must question themselves or their actions before speculating; how would this explosion of negative energy make this child or person feel? Energy must have a reasonable explanation and speak to whether the person is angry and out-of-control. It must also succinctly answer these questions:

Why is this happening?

What does it mean?

Am I losing control and/or do I need help?

For energy to be safe and wisely consumed, it must have boundaries and be balanced. Good energy must displace bad energy. Energy can neither be good nor bad, exclusively. Transferable energies that balance negative energies are a pleasing smile, a hug, a kiss, a touch, time taken or set aside, loving family members, role models, tutors, concerned neighbors, correction, loving discipline, rebuke that teaches, involvement, connection, recognition, affirmations, and/or assistance with problems.

Loving and caring parental involvement, at every stage of a child's growth, confirms within the mind of the child that they are safe and secure, and encourages the child's personal achievements. The loving environment of a secure family and home is so important that without it, during their formative years, personality, character, emotions, and/or the conduct of a growing child may be redirected into undesirable directions and behaviors. The absence of positive vocal and physical stimuli may cause the child to act out and/or experience low self-esteem and self-worth. As one grows into adulthood, these feelings may carry over and present as low personal confidence and discontentment with life. Parents must ensure the child has balanced energy, which is their lane.

As a parent, you have sheltered your children, fed them, clothed them, housed them, and sent them to a proper government-approved and sanctioned school facility. But, is this all that is needed to raise children beyond the level of just being human with needs akin to that of animals?

You have watched them grow, you have kept them entertained, and you have marveled at their ability to recall lyrics and knowledge. You have taken pride in their physical development, and spent your last dollar on their grooming. You have protected them from the outside elements, and from those that would have attached derogatory names, used negative connotations, and categorized them according to their sometimes seemingly out-of-control conduct. But as parents, have you equipped them to become more than just human flesh and blood; meat, moving headfirst into a pending slaughter?

Are you not aware that guns of some sort are waiting for your children? For too many, the only uncertainty is where the pending slaughter will take place. In the streets as anything but human, or more like animals butting their heads over who will gain the most and become the fattest, or maybe as nuisances to society counted with the undesirable, undervalued; only a number in an overcrowded stockade.

Children need your attention, Things are nice, but it is your attention, your time, and your presence that they need the most. Children may complain about what others have, and what they are wearing, but a loving arm and time spent together, before you take that much needed nap, is so important. Making sure you help them keep up with their classes, and making sure they have a dream that you are willing to buy into: can mean so much. Being the chief encourager, never letting them stay down when they are feeling down, and always willing to seek out sound remedies that will teach them how to overcome difficult times and situations... Yes, you guessed it... parents, this too is your lane.

Parents, the baton is in your hands. As lead runners, the parent must take time to mentor their child.

They must be intentionally focused and driven to prepare each child to become knowledgeable and well-adjusted participants in society. To simply feed, clothe, and house a child while we rush them to grow up is simply not enough. Even in the animal kingdom, it is unlikely that a mother will indulge her cubs until they grow to a certain size, and then simply leave them without survival skills, which include knowledge of jungle etiquette and respect for the hierarchy of their local pact.

In our civilized society, there are jungle-like elements waiting to slaughter the child. The ones who have been prepared can successfully negotiate the hurdles in society. Raising a child without instilling some navigational skills is akin to leaving your child in the wildlife of the human jungle environment to consume them. Children must be taught to strive for gold and not settle for less than that which they are capable of achieving. As they practice with their parent(s) for success, they must learn to be full distance runners, to run past the bling-bling of fake gold to achieve the real prize.

Whether on life's curves or straightaways, he/she must learn to adjust to changes while their footing remains sure. We cannot leave this wisdom training to our school systems, nor assume it will come from their gradual maturation. Well-adjusted and prepared adults stem from well-prepared and adjusted children. Adjusted teens will eventually become adjusted adults. The root and stem of this preparedness is centered in the parent's active involvement in every stage of the child's development.

Love must work arm-in-arm with knowledge, and responsibility, as parents actively interact, guide, and speak with their child or children. Boundaries must be set, and discipline wisely handed out. Respect must be the golden rule, and morals, like trees, must have deep roots, be implanted in his/her character, and exhibited in their conduct. Our system of government, which includes laws and law enforcement, must be explained, and held as fundamentally necessary for social order.

Just as in baton training, parents must labor to prepare each child to replace us at some point in life. The knowledge and skills acquired must be passed on to their child or children, who now run under the disciplines of social order, reflecting the character, judgments, and self-disciplines of their parents. Who in turn can be proud of the child/children they raised as representatives of the home in which they were raised! Children must be familiar with mental as well as physical exercises designed to strengthen their character and purpose for distance running. When these become attributes molded and shaped on the practice field, as teens and pre-teens; there is an excellent chance they will model what they have learned on the real track called, "life." As members and upcoming participants in the human race, each child must not only be strong enough to run but also know the disciplines of the race, and how to win within the confines of social order and etiquettes. There is only a short distance before they must be ready to run with what the parent has passed on to them! How the child has been raised, will determine how they get to the finish line and how they run their race. As parents, Mom and Dad; this is both of your lane!

It is real! It is the reason God created mankind. His desire for mankind to choose to be in relationship with Him and serve Him. That we would be intoxicated; high on Him. Every moment of our being, we should be drunk on His awesomeness. Our hearts should constantly overflow with His presence with an awareness of His love and provisions. The discovery of His vast universe and all that His hands have made specifically for humanity was to have kept us enraptured and connected to Him. As it was with the first man, Adam, there was to be an ever-present knowledge of the security that wrought in man a peace and satisfaction in the knowledge of God, our Creator.

This was evident in Adam's and God's relationship, where God would meet with Adam in the cool of the evening. Can you not see how overwhelming and exhilarating that must have been? Yet in the story of Cain and Abel, we find one brother experiencing immense joy in God, being pleased with his offering, while the other, from his choice not to conform to what would please God, found himself caught up in a spirit of hopelessness. So much so that he killed his brother. His turning from God's order and prerequisite to a way of his own brought about dissatisfaction within himself, and a strained relationship with his Creator, God. Subsequently, his life was filled with loneliness, fear, and considerable stress.

When man seeks his way apart from God, he loses sight of the presence of God, where there is "...the fullness of joy and pleasures for ever more..." (Psalms 16:11). As man's soul has spirit, he is created and intentionally programmed to relate spiritually to Him, who breathed the spirit of life into him, along with the purpose for his being. Without a personal God-Man relationship, man finds himself with an emptiness that he cannot, by his own means, fill or satisfy. Without divine fulfillment, all of man's toils lead to vanity and vexation of spirit. (Ecclesiastes 1-12). Man's labor becomes tiresome, and his accomplishment becomes futile. He is overwhelmed with his life; his faults and his gains are never enough. Therefore, the unbelieving, or disconnected man seeks to manufacture for himself what his inner man is crying for; a temporary relief, an escape; a utopian experience; a high that will take him beyond his inhibitions and allow him to float in a chemical land of make-believe where for a space in time he/she can avoid reality and all the negativity that has infiltrated and cluttered their minds.

Often, one's longing for this temporary escape becomes stronger than their ability or desire to live in the reality of life's experience. As sure as the serpent beguiled Eve by presenting her with a way that seems pleasing to man, this way also leads to destruction. Eventually, all enticed by its snare, are robbed of the substance of their labor, their sense of reasoning, their homes, families, and too often their lives. What appears as an escape is only another of Satan's tools to fulfill his purpose. Yep, to kill, steal, and destroy. These intoxicants chemically hijack and stimulate a reagent of the brain creatively designed to respond to heightened emotional conditions, such as joy, peace, and exceeding harmony between the mind of man and the spirit soul. These exhilarating feelings, when they occur, were solely intended to be intoxicating to the brain, creating various levels of rejoicing, happiness, and assurance, which often lead to emotional tears, shouting, or even uncontrollable dancing.

Recent health reports indicate that doctors verify the need for fulfillment in humankind, which comes from responding to an entity beyond themselves. They are now strongly pushing their findings, along with the rest of modern health advancements, to suggest that patients who exhibit feelings of hope, thankfulness, gratitude, and faith outside of themselves appear to trigger mental cell releases that affect the biochemical balance of the brain. Thereby, greatly improving the body's ability to heal and maintain a sense of wellbeing.

The Bible puts it this way:

"These things have I said unto you that my joy might remain in you, and that your joy might be complete." (Luke 15:11)

"The comforter which is the Holy Spirit whom the father will send in my name, He will teach you all things, and bring all things to your remembrance, whatsoever I have said unto you." (Luke 14:26)

"How the fruit of the Holy Spirit is love, joy, peace, long-suffering, gentleness, goodness, faith, meekness, and temperance, against such there is no law." (Galatians 5; 22)

This is your lane!

Pastor Parrott with over 50 Years as a bible student, completed his basic biblical studies at the FT. Wayne Bible College, Muncie Indiana Branch: under the direction of Dr. I. Broadus. Further studies in Sociology, Childhood Development, Apologetics, and Preaching etiquettes at Grace College, Warsaw Indiana. college campus.

His many years of personal study and teaching has enabled him to serve in several positions and capacities that include Young Adult as well as Adult Bible Studies, Sunday School Superintendent, Deacon, Pastor's Assistant, Assistant Pastor, Interim Pastor, and Pastor as a church pioneer.

Pastor Parrott has served as founder of Signs of Christ Ministry, before joining a ministry to the homeless called, "Hoot," where he served as Kitchen Director, Pantry Director, and Bible Study Leader, while serving on several other street ministry and Evangelistic team projects.

Pastor Parrott has founded several different ministries that include the ministry of Signs of Christ, Old Scholars Youth Rescue, and "Before They Strike, Stop The killing Ministries," that include the, "Back to Church," initiatives for the city of Indianapolis.

Pastor Parrott is currently serving in several capacities with Absolute Worship Ministries as a Bible Study Teacher, Minister ,and Minister's Development Leader, while assisting his pastor in whatever capacities he is needed. He is the writer of several papers on various topics and social issues including a Blog called, "RP Spiritual," and is now working on the second book titled, "In Need of a Man."

Old Scholars Youth Rescue

"To provide a reservoir of knowledge and wisdom from those who've been where our youth are."

Our Purpose

- To inject positive instructions from written and verbal knowledge that will reveal the snares, traps, consequences and escape routes from many of the conditions our youth find themselves facing today.
- To plant hope for a more positive future.

Our Mission

- To rally the mature adults of our society to ignite an active community concern that will move our city and state to address the challenges of our youth and confront the many negative influences of street survival and gun violence.

Before They Strike

We believe that the consequences and the reality of gun violence must be written-out and made plain, "before they strike."

Purpose and Objectives

- To prepare the mind to see and avoid the potential outcome of a confrontation.
- To be aware of and seek alternatives to the introduction of guns.
- To know the consequences of gun violence to self and others beforehand.
- To consider your tomorrow.

More information located at our website:
OldScholarsYouthRescue.org

www.ingramcontent.com/pod-product-compliance
Lightning Source LLC
LaVergne TN
LVHW020626100826
845148LV00012B/2069

9798988018605